Volume 24, Number 1, 2023

Quarterly Review OF Distance Education

RESEARCH THAT GUIDES PRACTICE

Editors:
Michael Simonson
Anymir Orellana

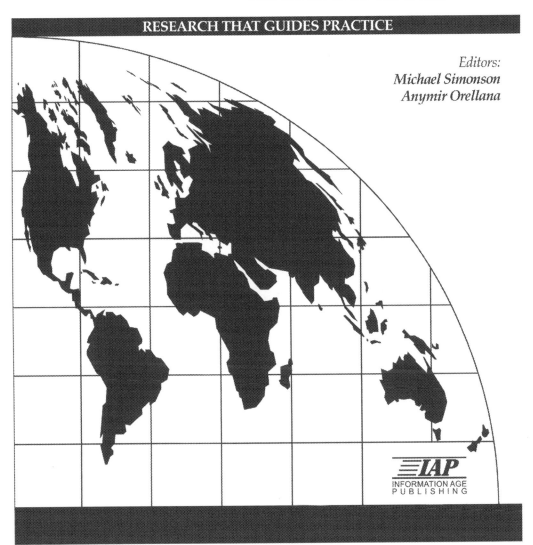

Quarterly Review of Distance Education
Editors and Editorial Board

Michael Simonson
Editor
Fischler College of Education and School of Criminal Justice
Nova Southeastern University
3301 College Avenue
Fort Lauderdale, FL 33314
800-986-3223 x8563
simsmich@nova.edu

Anymir Orellana
Editor
Fischler College of Education and School of Criminal Justice
Nova Southeastern University
3301 College Avenue
Fort Lauderdale, FL 33314
orellana@nova.edu

Charles Schlosser
Emeritus Editor

Vanaja Nethi
Assistant Editor
Nova Southeastern University

Alexander Martinie
Assistant to the Editors
Nova Southeastern University

Department Editors

Book Review
Shelly Wyatt

Social Media
Deborah Seepersaud

Copy Editor
Shirley Walrod

Editorial Board

Lee Ayers
Southern Oregon University

Ruth Gannon Cook
DePaul University School for New Learning

Michael Corry
George Washington University

Santanu De
Nova Southeastern University

Nabi Bux Jumani
International Islamic University

Gary Morrison
Old Dominion University

Anthony A. Piña
Illinois State University

Wilhelmina Savenye
Arizona State University

Christopher Thomas Miller
Morehead State University

Quarterly Review of Distance Education
"Research That Guides Practice"
Volume 24, Number 1, 2023

ARTICLES

Perceptions of Barriers to Learning Management Systems Among
Teaching English to Speakers of Other Languages Teachers
in Alabama and Mississippi
 Asmaa Benbaba and James Lindner *1*

Experiences in an Online Learning Community: The Student Perspective
 Michelle Wylie *15*

What the Debriefs Unfold: A Multicase Study of the Experiences
of Higher Education Faculty in Designing and Teaching
Their Asynchronous Online Courses
 Ritushree Chatterjee, Darshana Juvale, and Nadia Jaramillo Cherrez *25*

The Urbanization of Distance Education in Australia
 Chris Radcliffe *43*

Strategies for Managing the Challenges of Student Virtual Teams
in Higher Education: A Case Study
 Jill E. Nemiro, Anel Ayala, Jodee S. Lee, and Briseli San Luis *55*

BOOK REVIEWS

*Artificial Intelligence and Learning Futures: Critical Narratives
of Technology and Imagination in Higher Education,* by Stefan Popenici
 Reviewed by Rebecca McNulty *79*

*Hybrid-Flexible Course Design: Implementing Student-Directed
Hybrid Classes,* Edited by Brian J. Beatty
 Reviewed by Mohsen Keshavarz *83*

Conference Calendar
 Vanaja Nethi *87*

Author Biographical Data *91*

STATEMENT OF PURPOSE

The *Quarterly Review of Distance Education* is a rigorously refereed journal publishing articles, research briefs, reviews, and editorials dealing with the theories, research, and practices of distance education. The *Quarterly Review* publishes articles that utilize various methodologies that permit generalizable results which help guide the practice of the field of distance education in the public and private sectors. The *Quarterly Review* publishes full-length manuscripts as well as research briefs, editorials, reviews of programs and scholarly works, and columns. The *Quarterly Review* defines distance education as institutionally based, formal education, where the learning group is separated and where interactive technologies are used to unite the learning group.

DIRECTIONS TO CONTRIBUTORS

Submit your manuscript, typed double-spaced. Manuscripts are generally between 30 and 50 pages in length and must conform to the style of the most recent edition of the *Publication Manual of the American Psychological Association*. Longer manuscripts will be considered also. Research briefs may be shorter, normally between 3–10 pages.

The name(s), affiliation(s), address(es), and phone, fax, and email address(es) of the author(s) should appear on a separate cover page. A one-paragraph biographical statement should be submitted for each author.

To ensure anonymity in the review process, names of author(s) should not appear elsewhere in the manuscript, except in appropriate citations. An abstract of 100 words should also be submitted on a separate page.

Manuscripts should be submitted using a recent version of Microsoft Word. The file should be clearly labeled with the author(s) name(s). Graphics should be included as part of the Word document.

Manuscripts will be reviewed by at least three consulting editors. This process normally takes from 3–4 months.

Submit manuscripts using email to:

simsmich@nova.edu

Michael R. Simonson
Editor
Fischler College of Education and School of Criminal Justice
Nova Southeastern University
4118 DeSantis Building
3301 College Avenue
Fort Lauderdale, FL 33314

Name of Publication: ***Quarterly Review of Distance Education***
(ISSN: 1528-3518)
Issue: Volume 24, Number 1, 2023
Frequency: Quarterly

Office of Publication: IAP–Information Age Publishing, Inc.
P.O. Box 79049
Charlotte, NC 28271-7047
Tel: 704-752-9125
Fax: 704-752-9113
E-mail: QRDE@infoagepub.com
Web Address: www.infoagepub.com

Subscription Rates:
Institutions Print: $210.00
Personal Print: $95.00
Student Print: $65.00

Single Issue Price (print only): Institutions: $45.00, Personal $25.00
Back Issue Special Price (print only): Institutions $100.00;
Personal: $50.00; Student: $35.00
Outside the U.S. please add $25.00 for surface mail.

Editorial Office: *Quarterly Review of Distance Education*
Fischler College of Education and School of
Criminal Justice
Nova Southeastern University
3301 College Avenue
Fort Lauderdale, FL 33314
800-986-3223 ext. 8563
simsmich@nova.edu

Copyright © Information Age Publishing, Inc. 2023.

All rights of reproduction in any form reserved.

Quarterly Review of Distance Education is indexed
by the DE Hub Database of Distance Education.

PERCEPTIONS OF BARRIERS TO LEARNING MANAGEMENT SYSTEMS AMONG TEACHING ENGLISH TO SPEAKERS OF OTHER LANGUAGES TEACHERS IN ALABAMA AND MISSISSIPPI

Asmaa Benbaba
University of Kansas

James Lindner
Auburn University

This quantitative study aimed at investigating various barriers that hindered the diffusion of learning management systems (LMSs) as perceived by teaching English to speakers of other languages (TESOL) or English as a second language (ESL) teachers in the states of Alabama and Mississippi. A nonprobabilistic purposeful sampling was used in the selection of participants for this study ($N = 99$). Data were collected using an online questionnaire. The study determined the perceptions held by ESL/TESOL teachers about potential barriers to the adoption of LMSs in their online teaching. Results showed moderate barriers to the adoption of LMSs and concerns about time, planning, finances, technology, and incentives. The barriers with the highest levels were planning, time, and incentives.

INTRODUCTION

The increasing demand for studying the English language frequently requires teachers to meet the needs of a large population of English language learners (ELLs) from diverse backgrounds with various educational needs. Teaching English to speakers of other languages (TESOL) often entails teachers accepting and integrating innovation and change into

the learning process (Godwin-Jones, 2015). Several factors contributed to the shift to the latest innovations in teaching English as a second language (ESL). First, the emerging use of technological interventions in education at large through adopting online/hybrid learning has motivated change at the teaching and learning levels (Turnbull, 2010). Second, the fact that universities adopt learning management systems (LMSs), a trending technologi-

---

• **Correspondence concerning this article should be addressed to:** Asmaa Benbaba, asmaabenbaba@ku.edu

---

The Quarterly Review of Distance Education, Volume 24(1), 2023, pp. 1–13
Copyright © 2023 Information Age Publishing, Inc.

ISSN 1528-3518
All rights of reproduction in any form reserved.

cal innovation, implies that a set of responsibilities are added to the role of the ESL/TESOL, which leave educators unable to choose which platform to use for students' learning (Varghese & Jenkins, 2007). Third, the need to provide learners with more interactive skills has increased the need to promote teachers' performance to adopt a set of innovative teaching approaches and tools, including LMS environments.

Blackboard, Moodle, Desire2Learn, Schoology, and Canvas are leading LMSs (Salisbury, 2018). LMSs have been used in language teaching to create an online presence where learners can access and perform different learning activities. Examples are downloading files and notes to access the discussion boards, viewing short videos, and submitting quizzes and assignments (Blair & Hoy, 2006). An LMS is also used to support face-to-face course delivery (Coates et al., 2005), blended instruction, virtual training, and distance education (Dahlstrom et al., 2014).

THEORETICAL FRAMEWORK

For this research, the theoretical framework was drawn from Everett Rogers' (2003) Diffusion of Innovation. Rogers (2003) noted that "an innovation is communicated through certain channels over time among the members of a social system" (p. 5). Diffusing an innovation requires some mediums of communication (Rogers, 2003). Diffusion, according to Rogers (2003), is "a kind of social change" (p. 6) occurring in the structure of a social system. The diffusion rate is linked with how adopters perceive a specific innovation and its characteristics (Rogers, 2003). The perceived attributes of innovation are, therefore, a good explanation of the rate of adoption that happens over a specified time frame. Five attributes of innovations affect the adoption rate and impact the speed of its diffusion: relative advantage, compatibility, complexity, trialability, and observability (Rogers, 2003). Innovations with low complexity and high rel-

ative advantage, observability, trialability, and compatibility can diffuse quickly (Moore & Benbasat, 1991). Other factors, often called barriers, can negatively influence perceptions, the characteristics, and the rate of innovation diffused (Schifter, 2000). Teachers' adoption of LMSs increases when barriers are eliminated (Schifter, 2000; Tabata & Johnsrud, 2008). Similarly, facilitating conditions in teaching can encourage users' adoption of an innovation and reduce barriers (Panda & Mishra, 2007).

LITERATURE REVIEW

A literature review found significant studies (Hussein, 2011; Shea et al., 2005; Zhao et al., 2002) regarding barriers that may inhibit TESOL teachers from adopting a LMS. Barriers are operationally defined as negative influence factors on the perceptions and attitudes of the adopters of LMSs. The researcher for this study has identified five possible barriers based on the literature: time, incentives, finance, planning, and technology concerns (Betts, 1998). Myers et al. (2016) found that resistance to a new idea can hinder the adoption and diffusion of innovations (Wilcox et al., 2016). Obstacles to the adoption and diffusion of innovation can be related to "program credibility, administrative support, planning issues, technical expertise, financial concerns, concerns about time, concerns about incentives, infrastructure, conflict with traditional education, and fear of technology" (Li & Lindner, 2007, p. 47).

Other studies on teachers' perceptions of barriers to the diffusion of LMSs have shown that factors such as technical support, previous positive experience, course contents, and university departments' logistics affect faculty's perceptions and attitudes to integrating technology in the classroom (Shea et al., 2005). To examine the factors influencing the use of LMSs in Saudi Arabian higher education, Asiri (2012) identified and described some sets of external barriers that faculty members encountered. He classified them into three core categories: planning barriers, technological barriers and social barriers. Planning barriers are related to the organizational and logistic measures usually made to support technology in the classroom setting (Zhao et al., 2002). Al-Senaidi et al. (2009) explained that poor planning and technical support within public institutions are significant obstacles to faculty's adoption and use of Jusur LMS.

Hussein (2011) examined faculty members' attitudes at Saudi universities toward Jusur LMS. Results from the study revealed a set of positive attitudes toward Jusur LMS and three types of barriers: personal constraints, administrative constraints, and physical constraints (Hussein, 2011). According to Hussein, personal barriers refer to the strong resistance toward change or development in academia. Also, there is sometimes a need for more awareness about the importance of the integration of LMS, and therefore resistance to change emerges as an attitude toward the shift to distance education (Garrote, 2012).

Ottenbreit-Leftwich (2010) argued that teachers' beliefs about instruction tools indicate classroom use of technology (Ertmer & Ottenbreit-Leftwich, 2010). Ngai et al. (2007) indicated that facilitating conditions are enablers or barriers that impact a user's perception of simplicity or difficulty when carrying out a job. In a study investigating teachers' perceptions of library LMSs, results revealed the following barriers: the need for more awareness about the importance of the innovation, the lack of incentives, and the lack of training. These obstacles hinder faculty adoption and use of the library LMS tools (Leeder & Lonn, 2014).

Bennett and Bennett (2003) argued that teachers' perceptions of time spent learning how to teach using technology and the complexity of the innovation are major obstacles to not fully adopting instructional technologies. Researchers also agree that many types of instructional technologies require time for learning and teaching (Heijstra & Rafnsdottir, 2010). Introducing an innovation requires

more commitment to pedagogy (Benson & Palaskas, 2006). This situation makes faculty need help with the course's pedagogy and how to communicate the learning goals to the students by utilizing LMSs as an innovation. Such a process often takes time and effort to be effective (Reid, 2014). Instructional technologies such as LMSs have facilitated the shift to student-centered learning; however, Folkestad and Haag (2002) reported that faculty adopters perceive this as a disincentive and noted it necessitates more time compared with face-to-face instruction (Worley & Tesdell, 2009). Instructors are regarded as the first contact to whom students can report their LMS technical issues, which adds more workload on the teacher (Judge & O'Bannon, 2008).

Another barrier that impedes faculty's adoption of LMSs is legal concerns. All types of LMSs, such as Canvas, Moodle, or Blackboard, require instructors to upload class contents and materials into the online environment. This process involves ownership concerns, raising questions about copyright laws (McGrail & McGrail, 2010). Because the legal aspect of the online environment involves complex copyright regulations, faculty often express uncertainties and resistance by avoiding sharing class material online (Bruner, 2007). Universities do not treat online course materials as intellectual property, which creates a conflict of ownership among the academic community (Bruner, 2007).

Along with these challenges, incentive barriers can also inhibit the adoption of LMSs among faculty. The online environment has changed the role of the instructor, who is becoming both an instructor, a facilitator, and a technician of online courses via LMS. Such a shift in the roles, when not adequately supported by structure, training, and funding, can generate task concerns for adopters (Khan et al., 2015) and hinder innovation adoption. Online educators' need for compensation and recognition has regularly been identified as an obstacle for potential adopters (Muilenburg & Berge, 2009). Edwards and Minich (1998) found that most instructors needed to be recognized for their distance education times and efforts. Padilla and Terry (2010) argued that other types of incentives could motivate instructors to be invested in the innovation by "creating mechanisms to give faculty from different disciplines course credits for team teaching" (Hainline et al., 2010, p. 5). Feldstein (2017) argued that teachers would only remain motivated to spend time and effort if institutions provided some incentives. Wolcott (2001) explored faculty views on compensation and workload concerns and found that this population was more motivated by intrinsic factors than by extrinsic factors (Meyer, 2012). Betts (1998) noted that extrinsic factors are related to the intellectual challenge, personal drive to use technology, ability to reach out to a new population of students who cannot attend on-campus face-to-face classes, promotion, tenure, and recognition and reward. Intrinsic factors are related to the lack of release time, the lack of technical support, and the lack of clarity regarding workload. Intrinsic factors impact faculty participation in online education more than extrinsic factors (Betts, 1998).

PURPOSE

The purpose of this descriptive study was to describe teachers' perceptions of barriers to adopting LMSs (time, incentives, finance, planning, and technology). The findings presented in this article are part of a more extensive study that aimed to understand the influence of faculty perceptions about attributes and barriers influencing the diffusion of LMSs.

METHODS

The research presented in this study is part of a larger study that examined the influence of selected factors on the adoption of a LMS by TESOL) or ESL teachers. The target population was the faculty and teachers of TESOL in the states of Alabama and Mississippi. Very

few studies at the time of the research have examined the perceptions of LMSs among TESOL teachers in the states of Alabama and Mississippi. The target population was selected based on their role as leaders of their classes and part of communities of practice, adult educators, ESL teachers, and Intensive English Programs (IEPs) full-time and part-time instructors.

A nonprobabilistic purposeful sampling was used to select participants for this study, and the board of the Alabama-Mississippi Teaching English to Speakers of Other Languages (AMTESOL) permitted access to the population. The target population had 400 TESOL/ESL teachers (L. Preston, personal communication, May 14, 2019). Cochran's (1977) formula was used to estimate the sample size ($N = 99$). A questionnaire administered online was used to collect data. The instrument was based on research by Harder and Lindner (2007), who studied the diffusion of eXtension among the Cooperative Extension agents in the state of Texas (Harder, 2008; Li & Lindner, 2007). The instrument was used in several contexts to measure participants' perceptions when adopting innovations in agriculture.

Participants were asked to rate 28 statements on a 5-point summated scale, where 1 = *strongly disagree*, 2 = *disagree*, 3 = *neither agree nor disagree*, 4 = *agree*, and 5 = *strongly agree*. Harder (2007) proposed five constructs that this study has adopted: (a) financial concerns (4 items), (b) concerns about time (5 items), (c) concerns about incentives (6 items), (d) planning concerns (5 items), and (e) technology concerns (8 items). Under each construct, statements were modified based on Harder's (2007) instrument.

In a replicate study, Lindner and Harder (2007) previously tested the instrument's reliability, where $\alpha = .92$ (Cronbach, 1951). The instrument was adopted from Lindner and Harder (2007), where permission was obtained from J. Lindner (personal communication, August 20, 2018). Content validity was tested in the original instrument by a panel of experts composed of faculty members in the Department of Agricultural Education, Leadership, and Communications at Texas A&M University and the national marketing director of eXtension. The wording for several statements was modified and tailored to survey TESOL teachers and increase the possibility of obtaining valid and reliable results. Table 1 summarizes the number of items that this study did differently from Harder's (2007) number of items.

The questionnaires were emailed to (a) IEP directors working for the public system in Alabama and Mississippi, (b) IEP instructors in both states, (c) the TESOL International organization e-lounge, and (d) the Alabama-Mississippi Teaching English to Speakers of Other Languages. Email invitations to take the survey introduced the researcher, the research, and its importance, along with an attached letter of information, including the institutional research board permission to collect participant data. Data collection started on April 17, 2019, and ended on May 30, 2019. Nonresponders were reminded after 10 days of nonresponse. The total number of responses was 150, and the final sample size was ($N = 99$), with a 25% response rate. There were 51 responses removed because of incomplete or missing data.

RESULTS

This study describes teachers' perceptions of barriers to adopting LMSs by time, incentives, finance, planning, and technologies. Results show the means and standard deviations of the five barriers. The barriers that have higher values at the level of the mean were: planning ($M = 3.66$, $SD = 0.90$), time ($M = 3.54$, $SD = 0.96$), and incentives ($M = 3.53$, $SD = 0.91$). Barriers with lower mean values included technology concerns ($M = 3.47$, $SD = 0.81$) and financial concerns ($M = 3.48$, $SD = 0.98$). TESOL/ESL teachers from Alabama and Mississippi perceived all five constructs as moderate barriers to adopting LMSs.

CONCERNS ABOUT TIME

Five statements measured participants' perceptions about time concerns as a barrier to the adoption of a LMS. Table 2 displays the results, which were described by frequencies and percentages. Forty-eight point four percent of participants agreed or strongly agreed about time concerns accessing material in LMS. Forty-eight point four percent of participants indicated it was a strong or very strong barrier to responding to online requests through LMS, and 22 indicated it was moderate. As to the lack of time to meet students' needs, 57.2% of

TABLE 1

Reliability Levels of Internal Scales

Measures	Scale	Cronbach Alpha, as Described in Harder and Lindner (2008)	Harder's (2007) Number of Items by Construct (Items Adapted for This Research)
Concerns about time	5-point summative scale	.89	5 (5)
Concerns about incentives	5-point summative scale	.92	7 (6)
Financial concerns	5-point summative scale	.91	5 (4)
Planning concerns	5-point summative scale	.92	5 (5)
Technology concerns	5-point summative scale	.88	9 (8)

Note: Reliability levels ≥ .80 were considered acceptable (Harder, 2007; Harder & Lindner, 2008).

TABLE 2

Distribution of Participating ESL/TESOL Teachers by Their Perception of Concerns About Time as a Barrier to the Adoption of a LMS

T Time Concern Items	n	No Barrier		Weak Barrier		Moderate Barrier		Strong Barrier		Very Strongly Barrier	
		f	%	f	%	f	%	f	%	f	%
Lack of time available to access material in the LMS	91	2	2.2	25	27.5	20	22.0	19	20.9	25	27.5
Lack of time to meet the need of students using LMS	91	5	5.5	15	16.5	19	20.9	28	30.8	24	26.4
Lack of time to learn to incorporate LMS into job responsibilities	90	1	1.1	14	15.6	19	21.1	35	38.8	21	23.3
Lack of time available to respond to online request	91	2	2.2	25	27.5	20	22.0	19	20.9	25	27.5
Lack of time available to search for information on LMS	89	0	0	20	22.5	21	23.6	29	32.6	19	21.3

Note: Overall $M = 3.54$; $SD = 0.96$; scale: 1 = *no barrier*, 2 = *weak barrier*, 3 = *moderate barrier*, 4 = *strong barrier*, 5 = *very strongly barrier*; $n \neq 99$ due to item nonresponse.

participants indicated it was a strong or very strong barrier, while 20.9% indicated it was a moderate barrier.

As to the need for more time to learn how to incorporate LMSs into the typical jobs for teachers, 15.9% of participants indicated it was a weak barrier. In comparison, 62% indicated it was a strong or a very strong barrier. Regarding the lack of time to search for information on LMSs, 53.9% of participants indicated it was a strong or very strong barrier, and 23.6% indicated it was a moderate barrier. Overall, the mean and standard deviation for concerns about time as a perceived barrier to adopting LMSs were $M = 3.54$ and $SD = 0.96$. ESL/TESOL teachers tended to perceive time concerns as a moderate barrier.

CONCERNS ABOUT INCENTIVES

Participants' perceptions of concerns about incentives as a barrier to adopting LMSs were measured by participants' responses to five statements. Table 3 displays the responses' results described by frequencies and percent-

ages. Monetary compensation was indicated as a barrier to adopting LMSs, and 48.4% of participants indicated it was a strong or very strong barrier. The lack of institutional recognition can be a barrier to adopting LMSs, and 51% of respondents indicated it was a strong or very strong barrier. Participants indicated that the lack of correlation between a teacher's use of LMSs and teachers' evaluation could be a barrier. Over 20% of these participants indicated it was a very strong barrier, 27.5% revealed it was a strong barrier, and 39.6% indicated it was a moderate barrier.

Concerning the lack of rewards for involvement with LMSs, 33% believed it was a strong barrier and 24.2% indicated it was a very strong barrier, and 30.8% indicated it was moderate. The lack of monetary incentive for using LMSs was a barrier that hindered the adoption of LMSs. Forty percent indicated it was a strong barrier, and 24.2% stated it was a very strong barrier, while about 28.6% indicated it was a moderate barrier. Regarding the lack of time to search for information on LMSs, 24.2% indicated it was a strong barrier, whereas 15.4% indicated it was a very strong

Perceptions of Barriers to LMSs Among TESOL Teachers in Alabama and Mississippi 7

TABLE 3

Distribution of Participating ESL/TESOL Teachers by Their Perceptions of Concerns About Incentives as a Barrier to the Adoption of LMS

Inventive Concern Items	n	No Barrier		Weak Barrier		Moderate Barrier		Strong Barrier		Very Strongly Barrier	
		f	%	f	%	f	%	f	%	f	%
Lack of monetary compensation for using LMS	91	2	2.2	25	27.5	20	22.0	19	20.9	25	27.5
Lack of monetary incentive for using LMS	91	3	3.3	9	9.9	26	28.6	31	34.1	22	24.2
Lack of reward for involvement with LMS	91	4	4.4	7	7.7	28	30.8	30	33.0	22	24.2
Lack of correlation between use and evaluation of LMS	91	1	1.1	10	11.0	36	39.6	25	27.5	19	20.9
Lack of institution recognition for using LMS	91	5	5.6	14	15.6	25	27.8	29	32.2	17	18.9
Lack of time available to search for information on LMS	91	8	8.8	18	19.8	29	31.9	22	24.2	14	15.4

Note: Overall $M = 3.53$; $SD = 0.91$; scale: 1 = *no barrier*, 2 = *weak barrier*, 3 = *moderate barrier*, 4 = *strong barrier*, 5 = *very strongly barrier*; $n \neq 99$ due to item nonresponse.

barrier, and 31.9% of participants indicated it was a moderate barrier. In comparison, 19.8% indicated it was a weak barrier. Overall, the mean and standard deviation for concerns about incentives as a perceived barrier to adopting LMSs were $M = 3.53$ and $SD = 0.91$. ESL/TESOL teachers tended to perceive incentive concerns as a moderate barrier.

CONCERNS ABOUT PLANNING

As shown in Table 4, perceptions about planning issues as a barrier to adopting LMSs were measured by participants' responses to five statements. Regarding the lack of identified needs for LMSs, 19.8% of participants indicated it was a very strong barrier, whereas 33% indicated it was a strong one, and 26.4% indicated it was a moderate barrier. As for the need for a shared vision toward the role of LMSs with traditional institution structure, 35.2% of participants indicated it was a strong barrier,

25.3% indicated it was a very strong barrier, and 24.2% of indicated it was a moderate barrier. Regarding the need for more strategic planning for LMSs, 37.4% of participants indicated it was a strong barrier, and 25.3% believed it was a very strong one. In comparison, 22% indicated it was a moderate barrier.

Regarding the lack of coordination between LMS staff and faculty, 26.4% of participants indicated it was a very strong barrier, and 37.4% believed it was a strong one. In comparison, 20.9% indicated it was a moderate barrier. As to the lack of planned opportunities for teachers to learn about LMSs, 36.3% of participants indicated it was a strong barrier, and 25.3% believed it was a very strong barrier. Twenty-two percent of participants indicated it was a moderate barrier. Overall, the mean and standard deviation for planning issues as a perceived barrier to adopting LMSs were $M = 3.66$ and $SD = 0.90$. ESL/TESOL teachers tended to perceive planning issues as a moderate barrier to adopting LMSs.

TABLE 4

Distribution of Participating ESL/TESOL Teachers by Their Perception of Planning Concerns as a Barrier to the Adoption of LMSs

Planning Concern Items	n	No Barrier		Weak Barrier		Moderate Barrier		Strong Barrier		Very Strongly Barrier	
		f	%	f	%	f	%	f	%	f	%
Lack of coordination between LMS staff and faculty	91	1	1.1	13	14.3	19	20.9	34	37.4	24	26.4
Cost of strategic planning or LMS	91	1	1.1	13	14.3	20	22.0	34	37.4	23	25.3
Lack of opportunities to learn about LMS	91	2	2.2	13	14.3	20	22.0	33	36.3	23	25.3
Lack of shared vision with institution structure	91	2	2.2	12	13.2	22	24.2	32	35.2	23	25.3
Lack of identified needs for LMS	91	4	4.4	15	16.5	24	26.4	30	33.0	18	19.8

Note: Overall $M = 3.66$; $SD = 0.90$; scale: 1 = *no barrier*, 2 = *weak barrier*, 3 = *moderate barrier*, 4 = *strong barrier*, 5 = *very strongly barrier*; $n \neq 99$ due to item nonresponse.

FINANCIAL CONCERNS

Participants' perceptions about financial concerns as a barrier to the adoption of LMSs were measured by participants' responses to four statements. Table 5 displays the results, which were described by frequencies and percentages. As to the lack of funds to implement LMSs, 33% of participants indicated it was a strong barrier, and 17.6% indicated it was a very strong barrier. Twenty-two percent of participants indicated it was a moderate barrier. As to the lack of financial resources to support the necessary development of LMSs, 44% indicated it was a strong barrier, 17.6% indicated it was a very strong barrier, and 18.7% said it was a moderate barrier. For financial concerns about the resources to support necessary computer technology, 29.7% of participants indicated it was a strong barrier, whereas 20.9% believed it was a very strong barrier. Twenty-three percent of participants believed it was a moderate barrier. Thirty-four percent of participants indicated that the cost of purchasing the necessary computer technologies was a strong barrier, and 19.8% stated it was a very strong barrier. Also 24.2% indicated it was a moderate barrier. Overall, the mean and standard deviation for financial concerns as a perceived barrier to adopting LMSs were $M = 3.48$ and $SD = 0.98$. ESL/TESOL teachers tend to perceive financial concerns as a moderate barrier.

TECHNOLOGY CONCERNS

Participants' perceptions about technology issues as a barrier to the adoption of LMSs were measured by participants' responses to eight statements. Table 6 displays the results that were described by frequencies and percentages. As to the lack of teachers' access to LMSs, 30% of participants indicated it was a strong barrier, 14.4% indicated it was a very strong barrier, and 18.9% indicated it was a moderate barrier. As for the concern about the loss of important information when using LMSs, 29.7% of participants indicated it was a strong barrier, 17.6% indicated it was a very strong barrier, and 23% perceived it as a moderate barrier. As to the lack of teachers' access to technical support, 40% of participants indi-

Perceptions of Barriers to LMSs Among TESOL Teachers in Alabama and Mississippi

TABLE 5

Distribution of Participating ESL/TESOL Teachers by Their Perception of Financial Concerns as a Barrier to the Adoption of LMSs

Financial Concern Items	n	No Barrier		Weak Barrier		Moderate Barrier		Strong Barrier		Very Strongly Barrier	
		f	%	f	%	f	%	f	%	f	%
Lack of financial resources to support necessary development of LMS	91	2	2.2	16	17.6	17	18.7	40	44.0	16	17.6
Cost of purchasing the necessary computer technologies	91	0	0	20	22.0	22	24.2	31	34.1	18	19.8
Lack of funds to implement LMS on-site	91	2	2.2	23	25.3	20	22.0	30	33.0	16	17.6
Lack of financial resources to support necessary computer technology	91	1	1.1	23	25.3	21	23.1	27	29.7	19	20.9

Note: Overall $M = 3.48$; $SD = 0.98$; scale: 1 = *no barrier*, 2 = *weak barrier*, 3 = *moderate barrier*, 4 = *strong barrier*, 5 = *very strongly barrier*; $n \neq$ 99 due to item nonresponse.

TABLE 6

Distribution of Participating ESL/TESOL Teachers by Their Perception of Technology Concerns as a Barrier to the Adoption of LMSs

Financial Concern Items	n	No Barrier		Weak Barrier		Moderate Barrier		Strong Barrier		Very Strongly Barrier	
		f	%	f	%	f	%	f	%	f	%
Concerns about loss of face-to-face contact	90	2	2.0	12	13.3	19	21.1	30	33.3	27	30.0
Lack of training programs to learn to use LMS	90	2	2.2	15	16.7	17	18.9	33	36.7	23	25.6
Concern about intellectual property rights	91	2	2.2	16	17.6	19	20.9	35	38.5	19	20.9
Lack of teachers' access to technical support	90	5	5.6	15	16.7	20	22.2	36	40.0	14	15.6
Concern for legal issues (e.g., computer crime)	91	2	2.2	21	23.1	20	22.2	29	31.9	19	20.9
Concern about losing control of information	91	2	2.2	25	27.5	21	23.1	27	29.7	16	17.6
Concern that LMS will be used to replace teachers	91	7	7.7	20	20.0	21	23.1	19	20.9	24	26.4
Lack of teachers' access to LMS	90	5	5.6	28	31.1	17	18.9	27	30.0	13	14.4

Note: Overall $M = 3.47$; $SD = 0.81$; scale: 1 = *no barrier*, 2 = *weak barrier*, 3 = *moderate barrier*, 4 = *strong barrier*, 5 = *very strongly barrier*; $n \neq$ 99 due to item nonresponse.

cated it was a strong barrier, 15.6% indicated it was a very strong barrier, and 22.2% indicated it was a moderate barrier. Regarding legal issues, 31.9% of participants indicated it was a strong barrier, 20.9% believed it was a very strong barrier, and 22.2% indicated it was a moderate barrier.

Regarding the concern that LMSs would replace traditional teacher positions, about 20.9% of participants indicated it was a strong barrier, and 26.4% believed it was a very strong one. Twenty-three percent indicated it was a moderate barrier. Regarding intellectual property rights concerns, 38.5% indicated it was a strong barrier, and 20.9% believed it was a very strong barrier, while 20.9% indicated it was moderate. As for the lack of training programs to learn how to use LMSs, 36.7% indicated it was a strong barrier, and 25.6% believed it was a very strong barrier, while 18.9% indicated it was moderate. As to the concern about losing face-to-face contact with students, about 64% of participants indicated it was a strong and very strong barrier, and 21% indicated it was moderate. Overall, the mean and standard deviation for technology issues as a perceived barrier to adopting LMSs were $M = 3.47$ and $SD = 0.81$. ESL/TESOL teachers tended to perceive technology issues as a moderate barrier to adopting LMSs.

CONCLUSION, RECOMMENDATIONS, AND IMPLICATIONS

The study provided information that may contribute to addressing factors that impede the rate of adoption of LMSs. Alabama and Mississippi TESOL/ESL teachers perceived barriers to the diffusion of LMSs as moderate barriers. Planning concerns were perceived as the most significant barrier, and the concern about incentives was the second-largest concern on the list. The findings indicate that most participants agreed moderately with the five barriers identified by Rogers (2003) that would influence the diffusion of LMSs in Alabama

and Mississippi. All the items were perceived as moderate barriers to the diffusion of LMSs.

PERCEPTION OF TIME AS A BARRIER

Based on the perceived concerns about time as a potential barrier to the diffusion of LMSs, the study found that most TESOL/ESL teachers agreed with concerns about time as a potential barrier; 27.5% of the participants strongly agreed about time concerns accessing material via an LMS platform; 27.5% of participants agreed with the lack of time available to respond to online requests for information via LMSs; and 23.3% strongly agreed with the lack of time to learn how to incorporate LMSs into typical job responsibilities for teachers. Alabama and Mississippi TESOL/ESL teachers tended to perceive time concerns as a moderate barrier to the diffusion of LMSs. The findings confirm Bennett and Bennett (2003), who concluded that time is a major obstacle to not fully adopting instructional technologies such as LMSs. Teachers should be incentivized for the time they spend in LMSs.

PERCEPTION OF FINANCIAL CONCERNS AS A BARRIER

As to perceived financial concerns as a potential barrier to the diffusion of LMSs, results revealed that the majority of Alabama and Mississippi TESOL/ESL teachers moderately agreed with the existence of this barrier. Most participants were concerned about the need for more financial resources, funds, and the costs of securing necessary technologies. Forty-four percent of participants agreed that the lack of financial resources to support the necessary development of LMSs is a strong barrier, and 33% strongly perceive the lack of funds to implement LMSs as a barrier. The findings indicate that economic assessments may be needed to study why finances are considered barriers to the diffusion of LMSs. Alabama and Mississippi, public schools and university policy in both states need to be aware of the outcomes coming from the economic assessments of LMSs to decide whether provisions of financial resources translate to LMSs' long-term sustainability. Khan et al. (2015) conclude that the lack of funding can hinder the adoption of the innovation, which is a barrier.

PERCEPTION OF PLANNING CONCERNS AS A BARRIER

As to perceived planning concerns as a potential barrier to the diffusion of LMSs, this researcher found that the majority of Alabama and Mississippi teachers moderately agreed with the existence of this barrier, 37.4% of participants agreed that the lack of strategic planning for LMSs is a strong barrier, and 35.2% agreed that the lack of shared vision for the role of LMSs with traditional institution structure is a strong barrier. The findings indicate that the lack of identified needs for LMSs, the lack of shared vision for the role of LMSs, the lack of coordination between LMS staff and faculty, and the lack of strategic planning for LMSs all were seen as barriers that prohibit the diffusion of LMSs in Alabama and Mississippi. This finding agrees with Rogers (2003), who recognized that prerequisites and innovativeness were critical for an individual's innovation adoption behavior. Asiri (2012) confirmed that planning barriers related to the organization and logistic measures translate to a barrier to the adoption of LMSs.

PERCEPTION OF INCENTIVES AS A BARRIER

As to perceived concerns about incentives as a potential barrier to the diffusion of LMSs, this researcher found that the majority of TESOL/ESL teachers in Alabama and Mississippi agreed moderately with the existence of concerns about incentives as a potential barrier. Most participants were concerned about the lack of monetary incentives as a potential barrier to LMSs. More than 50% of participants

agreed with the following statements: (a) lack of monetary compensation for using LMSs; (b) lack of institutional recognition for using LMSs, and (c) lack of rewards for involvement with LMSs. The findings also confirm Muilenburg and Berge's (2009) findings that the lack of compensation and recognition in using an online platform has been identified as a barrier to LMSs.

PERCEPTION OF TECHNOLOGY CONCERNS AS A BARRIER

As to perceived technology concerns as a potential barrier to the diffusion of LMSs, the study found that the majority of TESOL/ESL teachers in Alabama and Mississippi moderately agreed with the existence of this barrier. A good majority of participants were concerned about possible complications derived from technology as a potential barrier. More than 50% of participants agreed with the following statements: (a) lack of training programs to learn about how to use LMSs; (b) concern for legal issues computer crime, hackers, software piracy, copyright), and (c) concern about intellectual property rights. The findings confirm McGrail and McGrails' (2010) statement that online platforms involve complex copyright regulations that teachers express uncertainties and resistance about. Ownership concerns are, therefore, a barrier.

REFERENCES

Asiri, M. J., Mahmud, R. B., Abu Bakar, K., & Mohd Ayub, A. F. Bin. (2012). Factors influencing the use of learning management system in Saudi Arabian higher education: A theoretical framework. *Higher Education Studies*, *2*(2), 125–137. https://doi.org/10.5539/hes.v2n2p125

Al-Senaidi, S., Lin, L., & Poirot, J. (2009). Barriers to adopting technology for teaching and learning in Oman. *Computers and Education*, *53*(3), 557–590. https://doi.org/10.1016/j.compedu.2009.03.015

Bennett, J., & Bennett, L. (2003). A review of factors that influence the diffusion of innovation when structuring a faculty training program. *Internet and Higher Education, 6*(1), 53–63. https://doi.org/10.1016/S1096-7516(02)00161-6

Benson, R., & Palaskas, T. (2006). Introducing a new learning management system: An institutional case study. *Australasian Journal of Educational Technology, 22*(4), 548–567. https://doi.org/10.14742/ajet.1285

Betts, K. S. (1998). An institutional overview: Factors influencing faculty participation in distance education in postsecondary education in the United States: An institutional study. *Online Journal of Distance Learning Administration, 1*(3), 1–14. https://www.westga.edu/~distance/betts13.html

Blair, K., & Hoy, C. (2006). Paying attention to adult learners online: The pedagogy and politics of community. *Computers and Composition, 23*(1), 32–48. https://doi.org/10.1016/j.compcom.2005.12.006

Bruner, J. (2007). Factors motivating and inhibiting faculty in offering their courses via distance education. *Online Journal of Distance Learning Administration, 10*(2), 36–59. https://www.westga.edu/~distance/ojdla/summer102/bruner102.htm

Coates, H., James, R., & Baldwin, G. (2005). A critical examination of the effects of learning management systems on university teaching and learning. *Tertiary Education and Management, 11*(1), 19–36. https://doi.org/10.1007/s11233-004-3567-9

Cochran, W. G. (1977). *Sampling techniques* (3rd ed.). John Wiley & Sons.

Cronbach, L. J. (1951). Coefficient alpha and the internal structure of the test. *Psychometrika, 16*(3), 297–334.

Dahlstrom, E., Brooks, D. C., & Bihchsel, J. (2014). *The current ecosystem of learning management systems in higher education: student, faculty, and IT perspectives* [Research report]. https://doi.org/10.13140/RG.2.1.3751.6005

Edwards, R., & Minich, E. (1998). *Faculty compensation and support issues in distance education: A study*. The Instructional Telecommunications Council.

Ertmer, P. A., & Ottenbreit-Leftwich, A. T. (2010). Teacher technology change: How knowledge, confidence, beliefs, and culture intersect. *Journal of Research on Technology in Education, 42*(3), 255–284. https://doi.org/10.1080/15391523.2010.10782551

Garrote, J. R. (2012). Barriers to a wider implementation of LMS in higher education : A Swedish case study, 2006–2011. *elected, 9*. https://eleed.campussource.de/archive/9/3371

Godwin-Jones, R. (2015). The evolving roles of language teachers: Training coders, local researchers, global citizens. *Language Learning & Technology, 19*(1), 10–22. https://eric.ed.gov/?id=EJ1051677

Hainline, L., Gaines, M., Feather, C. L., Padilla, E., & Terry, E. (2010). Changing students, faculty, and institutions in the twenty-first century. *Peer Review, 12*(3). https://www.aacu.org/publications-research/periodicals/changing-students-faculty-and-institutions-twenty-first-century

Harder, A., & Lindner, J. R. (2008). Characteristics and barriers impacting the diffusion of eXtension among Texas Cooperative Extension county extension agents. *Dissertation Abstracts International, 68*(9). (UMI No. 32810740)

Heijstra, T. M., & Rafnsdottir, G. L. (2010). The internet and academics' workload and work-family balance. *Internet and Higher Education, 13*(3), 158–163. https://doi.org/10.1016/j.iheduc.2010.03.004

Hussein, H. B. (2011). Attitudes of Saudi universities faculty members towards using the learning management system (JUSUR). *Turkish Online Journal of Educational Technology (TOJET), 10*(2), 43–53. https://eric.ed.gov/?id=EJ932224

Judge, S., & O'Bannon, B. (2008). Faculty integration of technology in teacher preparation: Outcomes of a development model. *Technology, Pedagogy, and Education, 17*(1), 17–28. https://doi.org/10.1080/14759390701847435

Khan, Z. R., Huda, N. N., & Mulani, V. (2015). Barriers and solutions to adopting blended-learning in private schools for students from low-income families. *E-Learning Excellence: Innovation Arabia, 8*, 472–494. https://ro.uow.edu.au/cgi/viewcontent.cgi?article=1700&context=dubaipapers

Leeder, C., & Lonn, S. (2014). Faculty usage of library tools in a learning management system. *College & Research Libraries, 75*(5), 641–663. https://doi.org/10.5860/crl.75.5.641

Li, Y., & Lindner, J. R. (2007). Faculty adoption behavior about web-based distance education: A case study from China Agricultural University. *British Journal of Educational Technology, 38*(1), 83–94. https://doi.org/10.1111/j.1467-8535.2006.00594.x

Meyer, K. A. (2012). The influence of online teaching on faculty productivity. *Innovative Higher Education*, *37*(1), 37–52. https://doi.org/10.1007/s10755-011-9183-y

Moore, G. C., & Benbasat, I. (1991). Development of an instrument to measure the perceptions of adopting an information technology innovation. *Information Systems Research*, *2*(3), 173–239. https://doi.org/10.1287/isre.2.3.192

McGrail, J. P., & McGrail, E. (2010). Overwrought copyright: Why copyright law from the analog age does not work in the digital age's society and classroom. *Education and Information Technologies*, *15*(2), 69–85. https://doi.org/10.1007/s10639-009-9097-9

Muilenburg, L., & Berge, Z. L. (2009). Barriers to distance education: A factor-analytic study. *American Journal of Distance Education*, *15*(2), 7–22. https://doi.org/10.1080/08923640109527081

Ngai, E. W. T., Poon, J. K. L., & Chan, Y. H. C. (2007). An empirical examination of the adoption of WebCT using TAM. *Computers and Education*, *48*(2), 250–267. https://doi.org/10.1016/j.compedu.2004.11.007

Panda, S., & Mishra, S. (2007). E-learning in a mega open university: Faculty attitude, barriers and motivators. *Educational Media International*, *44*(4), 323–338. https://doi.org/10.1080/09523980701680854

Reid, P. (2014). Categories for barriers to adoption of instructional technologies. *Education and Information Technologies*, *19*(2), 383–407. https://doi.org/10.1007/s10639-012-9222-z

Rogers, E. M. (2003). *Diffusion of innovations* (5th ed.). Free Press.

Salisbury, L. E. (2018). Just a tool: Instructors' attitudes and use of course management systems for online writing instruction. *Computers and Composition*, *48*, 1–17. https://doi.org/10.1016/j.compcom.2018.03.004

Schifter, C. C. (2000). Faculty motivators and inhibitors for participation in distance education. *Educational Technology*, *40*(2), 43–46. http://www.jstor.org/stable/44428591

Shea, P., Pickett, A., & Li, C. S. (2005). Increasing access to higher education: A study of the diffusion of online teaching among 913 college faculty. *International Review of Research in Open and Distance Learning*, *6*(2), 1–27. https://doi.org/10.19173/irrodl.v6i2.238

Tabata, L. N., & Johnsrud, L. K. (2008). The impact of faculty attitudes toward technology, distance education, and innovation. *Research in Higher Education*, *49*(7), 625–646. https://doi.org/10.1007/s11162-008-9094-7

Turnbull, M. (2010). There is a role for the l1 in second and foreign language teaching, but…. *Canadian Modern Language Review*, *57*(4), 531–540. https://doi.org/10.3138/cmlr.57.4.531

Varghese, M., & Jenkins, S. (2007). Challenges for ESL teacher professionalization in the US: A case study. *Intercultural Education*, *16*(1), 85–95. https://doi.org/10.1080/14636310500061948

Worley, W. L., & Tesdell, L. S. (2009). Instructor time and effort in online and face-to-face teaching: Lessons learned. *IEEE Transactions on Professional Communication*, *52*(2), 138–151. https://doi.org/10.1109/TPC.2009.2017990

Wilcox, A. K., Shoulders, C. W., & Myers, B. E. (2016). Encouraging teacher change within the realities of school-based agricultural education: Lessons from teachers' initial use of socioscientific issues-based instruction. *Journal of Agricultural Education*, *55*(5), 16–29. https://files.eric.ed.gov/fulltext/EJ1122771.pdf

Zhao, Y., Pugh, K., Sheldon, S., & Byers, J. L. (2002). Conditions for classroom technology innovations. *Teachers College Record*, *104*(3), 482–515. https://doi.org/10.1111/1467-9620.00170

EXPERIENCES IN AN ONLINE LEARNING COMMUNITY
The Student Perspective

Michelle Wylie
Chamberlain University

A descriptive qualitative design explored how graduate students in a master of public health program perceive the advantages and disadvantages of online learning communities and identified factors promoting graduation success. Zoom video and audio interview recordings from 12 participants were analyzed using Braun and Clarke's (2012) six-step thematic analysis. Six themes were developed: (1) time management; (2) self-motivation; (3) helping people in the community; (4) faculty engagement; (5) faculty discussion engagement; and (6) engagement outside the classroom. Students emphasized the importance of the faculty's presence in the online classroom, with personalized feedback and engagement in discussion boards as the central themes supporting students.

The field of public health is continually growing. Master of public health programs (MPH) emphasize the practical aspect of public health and the role of promoting community awareness, violence prevention, environmental awareness, communicable diseases, and other health and safety issues (Sullivan et al., 2018). There are 185 distance base programs, resulting in 84% of MPH degrees operating in the United States of America (Council on Education for Public Health, 2021). With the continual rise of programs and opportunities in the field, many people seek to switch careers with limited knowledge of the public health field or online education. However, online MPH programs need help with retention rates (Council of Education for Public Health, 2020). An informant of one program confirmed that "the MPH program has fallen short of the Council on Education for Public Health standard for three years" (C. Tex, personal communication, May 28, 2020).

There are three main stumbling blocks that students encounter. First, many of these MPH students are nontraditional graduate students who are either switching or trying to advance their careers in public health and are still determining what a degree in public health entails

---

• **Correspondence concerning this article should be addressed to:** Michelle Wylie, mwylie@chamberlain.edu

The Quarterly Review of Distance Education, Volume 24(1), 2023, pp. 15–23
Copyright © 2023 Information Age Publishing, Inc.

ISSN 1528-3518
All rights of reproduction in any form reserved.

(Sullivan et al., 2018). Second, most online MPH graduate students face constraints such as raising families and outside employment, which makes the programs challenging and demanding. Third and finally, students starting MPH classes are from various backgrounds and struggle with writing assignments in the classroom (Sullivan et al., 2018). Online learning offers valuable benefits to these nontraditional MPH graduate students.

Online education provides a form of graduate education with a flexible schedule that enables nontraditional students to expand their educational potential in the comfort of their homes (Lee, 2017). Martin et al. (2017) conducted a content analysis of existing global online learning standards to identify essential standards for success in online graduate education. Course designers have applied these seven principles: (a) access to the instructor, (b) cooperation with peers, (c) active learning interventions, (d) prompt feedback, (e) timely tasks, (f) constant communication, and (g) respect for different ways of learning to the development of online courses with positive results (Martin et al., 2017). The most important standards were satisfaction, instructor support, policies, and planning (Baldwin & Trespalacios, 2017). Therefore, online education provides graduate education with a flexible schedule that enables nontraditional students to expand their educational potential in the comfort of their homes (Lee, 2017). However, online learning also generates areas of challenges for creating a community.

Community, described as a feeling of being part of a social group, is critical to online students' success (Berry, 2018). In the face-to-face classroom, students foster community by sitting in one room and looking at facial cues and body language. An online learning community fosters a connection among students through working together in a trust-based atmosphere (Baran, 2019). Students who feel connected to the instructor and peers are more engaged in the online learning environment and less likely to withdraw from the program (Gillett-Swan, 2017). Therefore, the problem explored by this study concerns the inconsistent implementation of online learning communities, which may negatively influence graduate school students' success.

The study's conceptual framework was Siemens's (2004) connectivism theory. The theory of connectivism is rooted in several cognitive learning theories. Behaviorism, cognitivism, and constructivism are theories that frame learning approaches and best practices for use with students (Siemens, 2017). A key topic of the connectivism theory is the importance of learning within a community setting to promote knowledge sharing, collaboration, and students assisting one another when confronted with complex material (Goldie, 2016). Students learn what knowledge is by drawing inferences, connecting to, and participating in learning communities (Goldie, 2016). In addition, students can engage with each other in conversation, as these conversations in an online classroom are part of the discussion with images, videos, and multimedia, allowing the students to learn (Goldie, 2016).

PURPOSE OF THE STUDY

This study explored an area of higher education that has the potential to assist online graduate education practitioners. In addition, the study aimed to understand the perceived impact of implementing online learning communities.

The study explored graduate students' perceptions in an online university and discerned how participation within a virtual learning community could impact learning outcomes. The guiding research questions were:

Research Question 1: How do graduate students in an online master of public health program perceive the efficacy of online learning communities?

Research Question 2: Which components of online learning communities do graduate students in an online master of public health program perceive as most beneficial to graduate student success?

The study contributes to the limited research on best practices for implementing online learning communities within higher education, particularly graduate education. The study could also aid in understanding how online learning communities impact graduate students' outcomes. The study examined the perceived advantages and disadvantages of online learning communities. In addition, the study was developed to create positive social change by identifying factors that promote student success to help students graduate.

METHODOLOGY

This study used qualitative methodology and a descriptive qualitative design (Sandelowski, 2000) to interview a convenience sample of 12 students in a postsecondary university enrolled in an MPH program. The university used as the study site is a private for-profit healthcare and nursing school with campuses across the United States that also offers online programs. The Higher Learning Commissions accredit the university with a master of public health, master of social work, and doctor of nursing practice. The analysis used Braun and Clarke's (2012) six-step thematic analysis process to analyze the data collected from Zoom video and audio recordings and identify overarching themes in the data.

Participant Profiles

Convenience sampling was used to obtain the participants. Site approval was obtained from the dean of students for the program, and a list of potential participants was obtained for initial contact for the study. The participants for this study were 12 master of public health students currently enrolled in the program. All students were women in the field of public health. Of the 12 students, nine (75%) had prior online educational experience with their undergraduate courses or professional development classes. Three students (25%) were taking online courses for the first time. Additionally, all 12 graduate students were working professionals, 7 of whom were mothers.

Instrumentation

The research instrument, its development, and the subsequent data analysis were related to the literature review and the theory of connectivism that comprised the study's framework. This research resulted in 10 semistructured questions using further probing questions targeted at the 12 students from the master of public health online program. The questions were grouped into categories, including (a) engagement in the classroom, (b) perceptions of the efficacy of online learning communities, (c) feelings of isolation and aloneness, and (d) their overall experiences in the online program. Probing questions were used to clarify participant responses and obtain additional information on specific points.

Data Collection

Volunteer participants responded to the email, and individual virtual interviews were conducted conveniently for each participant's schedule via the Zoom.us virtual platform (Zoom Video Communications Inc., 2016). The interviews took place before work hours, during lunch breaks, and after work to not interfere with the participants' employment commitments. Informed consent was obtained before the interview commenced. The interviews were between 30–45 minutes in length. I also jotted down notes of the student's feelings or personal biases during the interview.

Data Analysis

Interviews from 12 participants were coded and analyzed by hand using Microsoft Excel spreadsheets as a framework. The use of Microsoft Excel also supported a deductive coding process. The deductive approach was chosen due to the theoretical framework used for the study and a priori codes developed for the interview questions (Christians et al., 1989). The data analysis process was conducted using Braun and Clarke's (2012) six-step approach to thematic analysis.

According to Braun and Clarke, the first step in the six-step process is to review the text several times in preparation for the initial coding process. The a priori codes provided high-level codes for initially grouping text sections that responded to the interview questions in step two. Step two also encourages coding as an iterative process. Following these steps, the information was coded further by reviewing the answers to 10 semistructured and five probing interview questions and relating the answers to the initial a priori codes. As the initial coding progressed, additional high-level codes were developed to capture the descriptions and thoughts of the participants.

In the third step, additional codes were developed for the segmented text once the interview text was segmented into blocks under the high-level codes. In this step, I identified codes and highlighted the text, allowing me to see the reoccurring codes with the specific response from the interview text. The reoccurring codes were then transferred to an additional Microsoft Excel sheet for comparison, categorization, and reorganization.

This process led to step four, where the reoccurring codes were compared across the data sets, and initial categories and themes were developed. Then, using the identified codes, I could figure out the relationship between the codes. In the fifth step, these themes were refined through an iterative analysis process. The sixth and final step involved developing the final analysis of the data. Table 1 lists the final themes.

FINDINGS

Six themes were generated from the data. This section discusses the significant contribution of the study findings to the scientific body of knowledge by addressing the research questions. Research question one asked: How do graduate students in an online master of public health program perceive the efficacy of online learning communities? The results indicated that graduate students perceive online learning communities as effective. Three themes emerged to respond to the issue of efficacy. The first theme concerned time management and how the program supported and required this skill for graduate students. The second theme concerned the self-motivation of graduate students to succeed in the program. The third theme indicated that helping people in the community was also seen as a motivation for success.

Research Question 2 asked which components of online learning communities graduate students in an online master of public health program perceive as most beneficial to graduate student success. The results indicated that three key issues are beneficial to graduate stu-

TABLE 1

Final Themes Answering the Research Questions

Research Questions	Final Themes
• **RQ1:** How do graduate students in an online master of public health program perceive the efficacy of online learning communities?	• Theme 1. Time management • Theme 2. Self-motivation • Theme 3. Helping people in their community
• **RQ2:** Which components of online learning communities do graduate students in an online master of public health program perceive as most beneficial to graduate student success?	• Theme 4. Faculty engagement • Theme 5. Faculty discussion engagement • Theme 6. Engagement outside the classroom

dent success. The first theme discussed the issue of faculty engagement with the online MPH student. The second theme specified the online discussion engagement of the faculty with the online MPH graduate student. Finally, the third theme concerned the importance of engagement outside the online classroom for the online MPH program.

Theme 1. Time Management

All 12 graduate students struggled with time management. Their need to balance everything between home, work, and life was overwhelming. Added to these needs was figuring out how to accomplish their schoolwork. The graduate students explained that figuring out how to manage online school and life took time. Respondents 1, 4, and 8 all expressed how managing their day-to-day tasks and adding schoolwork overwhelmed them.

Theme 2. Self-Motivation

The 12 graduate students also all had a strong desire to succeed in their schoolwork due to their personal desires to succeed in their careers. The graduate students also expressed their desire to receive a master's degree, and that goal helped them be successful in the classroom.

Theme 3. Helping People in Their Community

Two graduate students expressed their desire to help their community lead healthier lifestyles by learning about public health. These graduate students' desire to change their community helped them challenge themselves in the classroom, knowing they could make a difference in their communities.

Theme 4. Faculty Engagement

Faculty engagement is a strong theme essential to these graduate students' success in the classroom. The faculty reaching out and engaging with the graduate students through phone calls, text messages, and emails help the graduate students know that the faculty is invested in the classroom and their success.

Theme 5. Faculty Discussion Engagement

Faculty discussion engagement is critical to the success of the graduate student. MPH instructors and graduate students must work collaboratively to create a sense of belonging, promoting MPH graduate student engagement and success in the virtual environment (Sullivan et al., 2018). When the faculty provided personalized and insightful discussion responses, it helped the graduate students to learn the public health material and foster educational improvement. In addition, when the faculty provides personalized feedback, that allows the graduate student to feel that the faculty are engaged in the classroom and learning the material.

Theme 6. Engagement Outside the Classroom

Engagement in groups, the new student orientation, town halls, and the master of public health Student group were essential to the graduate student's engagement and success in the online MPH program. In addition, other supportive events were mentioned, such as forming study groups and connecting with graduate students outside the classroom.

DISCUSSION

These results support the importance of online learning communities to master of public health graduate students. In addition, these findings support research from the literature review indicating that a flexible schedule enables nontraditional students to succeed in online learning communities (Lee, 2017). Baldwin and Trespalacios (2017) stated that the essential standards associated with online learning that all 12 graduate students expressed in instructor support interviews were vital to their academic success. The graduate students also expressed seven principles of Martin et al. (2017): (a) access to the instructor, (b) cooperation with peers, (c) active learning interventions, (d) prompt feedback, (e) timely tasks, (f) constant communication, and (g) respect for different ways of learning to the development of online courses with positive results. Through the different interviews, these seven principles clarified that the graduate students found these themes important in their success.

Theme 1. Time Management

These views were addressed in the Mental Health and Online Learning literature review of how students struggle to maintain balance in the online classroom and life. Online MPH programs must consider how these graduate students maintain and juggle school, home, and life. Two of these considerations are setting up online support resources to connect with faculty to get instant feedback. Having chat features to connect with graduate students online will help them stay connected to the faculty and their peers. Understanding the nontraditional MPH perspective of the emerging themes will help Deans and faculty make positive changes in the curriculum (Lang, 2019).

Theme 2. Self-Motivation

This topic was not addressed in the literature review but is an important theme to continue researching. The 12 graduate students also all had a strong desire to succeed in their schoolwork due to their personal desires to succeed in their careers. The graduate students also expressed their desire to receive a master's degree, and that goal helped them be successful in the classroom.

Theme 3. Helping People in Their Community

This topic was not addressed in the literature review but is an important theme to continue researching. Two graduate students expressed their desire to help their community lead healthier lifestyles by learning about public health. These graduate students' desire to change their community helped them challenge themselves in the classroom, knowing they could make a difference in their communities.

Theme 4. Faculty Engagement

This issue was discussed in the literature review under the topics of social presence in the online classroom and effective teaching strategies for the online classroom. The actions that create a sense of belonging in the classroom for the graduate students can assist the faculty with engaging and supporting the graduate student's success (Berry, 2017). Thus, this finding is supported by the literature on online MPH programs. Further, this finding indicates that MPH graduate programs must adapt procedures for faculty to engage with their graduate students in the classroom.

Theme 5. Faculty Discussion Engagement

Faculty discussion engagement was discussed in the literature review through feedback use in the online classroom. Graduate students thrive on the personalized feedback that faculty provide them. Online MPH graduate programs may need to adapt these recommendations to help graduate students succeed in the classroom. In educational contexts, instructors, learners, and peers join to form what is typically considered a community of practice (Arasaratnam-Smith & Northcote, 2017). Bowers and Kumar (2015) indicated that students strongly connect with their instructors within these communities. Creating a sense of belonging in the online classroom is

Experiences in an Online Learning Community

a crucial topic of interest related to online learning and helps overall student outcomes and satisfaction (Berry, 2017). Students within a community of practice feel a strong connection with their instructors (Bowers & Kumar, 2015; Voelkel & Chrispeels, 2017). Establishing strong connections with their faculty through discussion engagement will help graduate students be successful.

Theme 6. Engagement Outside the Classroom

Arasaratnam-Smith and Northcote (2017) stated that students need to feel a sense of belonging when interacting in online communities. This engagement must start when the student joins a program and is assigned to a cohort. MPH programs must support and encourage students to attend the new student orientation, town halls, and the master of public health student groups. These groups will support engagement in online communities Arasaratnam-Smith and Northcote (2017) also explored the concept of constant communication and its significance for creating a community of practice online. Having opportunities for graduate students to connect outside the classroom with their faculty and peers will help the graduate students feel connected to the classroom.

PRACTICAL IMPLICATIONS

The results of this study could be used by academic leadership to help implement curriculum plans to enhance graduate student engagement in MPH programs. Academic leadership may consider the graduate student perceptions of the master of online programs informative of how to make changes within their programs to enhance graduate student retention. Involving the graduate student perspectives in modeling faculty responsibility in providing important individual feedback, video lectures, and availability to meet with graduate students will help enhance student

retention in the program. Incorporating the graduate student's perceptions and the faculty's ideas and suggestions for improvement will help understand how to create an engaging community in the online classroom.

LIMITATIONS

There were five main limitations to this study. These limitations were related to the participants, research site, coronavirus pandemic, methodological weakness, and researcher bias. The first limitation of the study was the possibility of finding graduate students willing to participate. Although additional graduate students may have wished to participate, they may have needed to drop out of the study due to health, financial issues, or changing jobs. The second limitation was that the results were not generalizable to all institutions because only one group from a specific institution was being investigated. I interviewed 12 graduate students based on the program's size from which I drew the sample. However, the limited sample of respondents was sufficient for a qualitative study and reached data saturation. The third limitation was that the COVID-19 Pandemic left many graduate students feeling even more uneasy and lonely in life than before. The sensitive nature of questions about isolation and potential anxiety was carefully addressed. If a participant seemed distressed, I ended the interview and helped to provide them with information related to mental health and psychological help. The fourth limitation was that methodological weakness related to notetaking, transcription, and the transfer of the information to computer programs may have occurred. Human error can occur in notetaking or the coding of the data. The notes may not give full details about the responses, which may have affected the coding of the responses. The fifth limitation was potential researcher biases, including my history and involvement with MPH programs and the opinions and interpretations I have accumulated. I guarded against personal bias during the study by not having any prior contact with the graduate students before the study. Addressing these limitations was essential to ensure neutrality and professionalism throughout the research's data collection and analysis phases. I worked to gain trust and confidentiality with the participants in this study.

FURTHER RESEARCH

I recommend that this study be replicated in MPH programs and other online master programs across the United States to understand graduate student perceptions of online MPH programs. Including current graduate students and alums would add depth and variety for additional information. In addition, a replication of this study could help by identifying factors that promote graduate student success to support retention and to help students graduate. Understanding the graduate student's perspective can help the administration understand the changes to their curriculum or incorporate opportunities for students to connect virtually. I also recommend a comparative study of the faculty's perception of the initiatives they have been working on to help foster engagement and inclusion in the online classroom. This comparative study could also be done at other online master's programs to learn how their graduate students can foster engagement and inclusion in the online classroom.

Acknowledgment: No outside support was provided for this study.

REFERENCES

Arasaratnam-Smith, L. A., & Northcote, M. (2017). Community in online higher education: Challenges and opportunities. *Electronic Journal of E-Learning, 15*(2), 188–198. https://files.eric.ed.gov/fulltext/EJ1141773.pdf

Baran, E. (2019). *Rovai, "A practical framework for evaluating online distance education programs."* Online Learning Toolbox. https://iastate.pressbooks.pub/onlinelearningtoolbox/chapter/rovai-a-practical-framework-for-evaluating-online-distance-education-programs/

Bowers, J., & Kumar, P. (2015). Students' perceptions of teaching and social presence: A comparative analysis of face-to-face and online learning environments. *International Journal of Web-Based Learning and Teaching Technologies, 10*(1), 27–44.

Braun, V., & Clarke, V. (2012). Thematic analysis. In H. Cooper, P. M. Camic, D. L. Long, A. T. Panter, D. Rindskopf, & K. J. Sher (Eds.), *APA handbook of research methods in psychology, Vol. 2: Research designs: Quantitative, qualitative, neuropsychological, and biological.* American Psychological Association.

Christians, C. G., & Carey, J. W. (1989). The logic and aims of qualitative research. In G. H. Stempel III & B. H. Westley (Eds.), *Research methods in mass communication* (pp. 354–374). Prentice-Hall.

Clark-Gordon, C. V., Bowman, N. D., Watts, E. R., Banks, J., & Knight, J. M. (2018). "As good as your word": Face-threat mitigation and the use of instructor nonverbal cues on students' perceptions of digital feedback. *Communication Education, 67*(2), 206–225. https://doi.org/10.1080/03634523.2018.1428759

Council of Education for Public Health. (2020). *Council of Education annual report.* https://ceph.org

Gillett-Swan, J. (2017). The challenges of online learning: Supporting and engaging the isolated learner. *Journal of Learning Design, 10*(1), 20. https://doi.org/10.5204/jld.v9i3.293

Goldie, J. G. S. (2016). Connectivism: A knowledge learning theory for the digital age? *Medical Teacher, 38*(10), 1064–1069. https://doi.org/10.3109/0142159X.2016.1173661

Kumar, A., Kumar, P., Palvia, S. C. J., & Verma, S. (2017). Online education worldwide: Current status and emerging trends. *Journal of Information Technology Case and Application Research, 19*(1), 3–9. https://doi.org/10.1080/15228053.2017.1294867

Lang, T. A. (2019). Who me? Ideas for faculty who never expected to be teaching public health students to write. *Public Health Report, 134*(2), 206–214. https://doi.org/10.1177/0033354918821880

Lee, K. (2017). Rethinking the accessibility of online higher education: A historical review. *The Internet and Higher Education, 22,* 15–23.

Martin, F., Polly, D., Jokiaho, A., & May, B. (2017). Evaluation instruments and good practices in online education. *The Quarterly Review of Distance Education, 18*(2), 1–10. https://olj.onlinelearningconsortium.org/index.php/olj/article/view/913

Nguyen, V. A. (2017). The impact of online learning activities on student learning outcome in blended learning course. *Journal of Information & Knowledge Management, 16*(4), 1750040. https://doi.org/10.1142/s021964921750040x

QSR International. (2021). Nvivo Qualitative Software. https://www.qsrinternational.com/nvivo-qualitative-data-analysis-software/home

Sandelowski, M. (2000). Whatever happened to qualitative description? *Research in Nursing & Health, 23*(4), 334–340. https://doi.org/10.1002/1098-240x(200008)23:4<334::aid-nur9>3.0.co;2-g

Siemens, G. (2004). *Connectivism: A learning theory for the digital age.* Elearnspace. http://www.elearnspace.org

Siemens, G. (2017). Connectivism. In *Foundations of learning and instructional design technology.* Pressbooks. https://lidtfoundations.pressbooks.com/chapter/connectivism-a-learning-theory-for-the-digital-age

Sullivan, L. M., Velez, A., Edouard, V.B., & Galea, S. (2018). Realigning the master of public health (MPH) to meet the evolving needs of the workforce. *Pedagogy in Health Promotion, 4*(4), 301–311. https://doi.org/10.1177/2373379917746698

U.S. Bureau of Labor Statistics. (2020, September 1). *Healthcare occupations: Occupational outlook handbook.* U.S. Bureau of Labor Statistics. https://www.bls.gov/ooh/healthcare/home.htm

Voelkel, R. H., & Chrispeels, J. H. (2017). Understanding the link between professional learning communities and teacher collective efficacy. *School Effectiveness and School Improvement, 28*(4), 505–526. https://doi.org/10.1080/09243453.2017.1299015

Zoom Video Communications Inc. (2016). Security guide. https://d24cgw3uvb9a9h.cloudfront.net/static/81625/doc/Zoom-Security-White-Paper.pdf

WHAT THE DEBRIEFS UNFOLD
A Multicase Study of the Experiences of Higher Education Faculty in Designing and Teaching Their Asynchronous Online Courses

Ritushree Chatterjee, Darshana Juvale, and Nadia Jaramillo Cherrez
Iowa State University

This multicase study describes the unique experiences of online instructors within a novel context of grant-funded online course design assistance in a large Midwestern university. Five instructors reflected on their experience, from conception to implementation of their asynchronous online courses, in individual debrief sessions conducted by the instructional designers of the courses. Such reflections helped both, the instructors and the instructional designers, to better understand the design process potentially leading to more effective online course designing and implementation experiences, processes, and practices.

Online learning has revolutionized educational practices with new paradigms, pedagogies, and technologies employed to design courses that enhance student learning experiences. It provides higher education institutions with a low-cost, flexible way to reach a global audience (Casey, 2008). According to Allen and Seaman (2018), enrollment in distance education has increased for the 14th consecutive year in the United States, growing faster than ever before. Around 16.7% of students are at least taking one distance learning course. The 13th Babson Report (Allen & Seaman, 2016, p. 3) on online learning states that "When more than one quarter of higher education students are taking a course online, distance education is clearly mainstream."

During the past year, when the world was struck by the catastrophic COVID-19 pandemic, online and distance learning played a critical role in providing opportunities for continuous learning in higher education contexts (Dhawan, 2020; Misra & Chauhan, 2020). Undoubtedly, online learning in higher education will play a more significant role in the coming years.

However, for this mode of learning to be successful, it is of utmost importance to design

---

• **Correspondence concerning this article should be addressed to:** Ritushree Chatterjee, ritushree.chatterjee@gmail.com

The Quarterly Review of Distance Education, Volume 24(1), 2023, pp. 25–41
Copyright © 2023 Information Age Publishing, Inc.

ISSN 1528-3518
All rights of reproduction in any form reserved.

learner-centric online courses that promote interaction, engagement, a sense of belonging, and community while allowing students to succeed in their learning goals. Jaggars and Xu (2016) explored four areas that impact student performance and satisfaction in an online course, namely (a) organization and presentation, (b) learning objectives and assessments, (c) interpersonal interaction, and (d) use of technology. Among these four parameters, the one that stood out and had the most impact on student performance was interpersonal interaction—specifically, frequent and effective student-instructor interaction (Jaggers & Xu, 2016). This finding brings us to the critical role that online instructors play in the successful delivery of an online course and in the design of online learning environments.

In the online context, the role of the instructor has been redefined and is multidimensional. Throughout the duration of an online course, the instructor has to adapt and change their roles from being a planner to a model, coach, facilitator, and communicator (Huer & King, 2004). However, an instructor's impactful role is observed during the developmental stages of an online course when they plan, organize, and structure the course (Baran et al., 2011). These developmental tasks are considered one of online instructors' most important course design responsibilities.

The course design directly impacts student satisfaction; more structured/organized courses, more interaction, and collaboration and reflection opportunities lead to higher student satisfaction and performance (Kauffman, 2015). Baldwin et al. (2018) proposed a model to illustrate the course design process adopted by online instructors. He called it the Informal Design Theory, representing a dynamic problem-solving approach to the online course design process. They further articulated the need for a better understanding of this course design process to understand the instructor's needs.

Our study delves into this aspect of online learning—the need to understand the experiences and processes of an instructor during the planning and implementation stages of an online course. To this end, a series of debriefs with instructors were conducted to understand how they adopted a course design process. For the context of this paper, the debriefs are a series of semistructured interviews conducted individually with each instructor after the first offering of their online course. This study presents the instructors' stories that these debriefs helped unfold to better understand the instructors' experiences and pedagogical needs for course development assistance. This understanding will help identify strategies and procedures to assist with those needs that will ultimately enhance the learning experience for the learner.

The following sections of the paper will elaborate on the context of the study, the conceptual framework, the research design, and the methodology, along with elaborating on the findings of the debriefs.

CONTEXT

The study was conducted within the online learning unit housed in the colleges of engineering (COE) and liberal arts and sciences (LAS) at a large land-grant research university in the Midwest of the United States. The online learning unit awards grants (financial support) to instructors to design and develop their asynchronous online and blended courses. Grant-recipient instructors work collaboratively with a highly skilled instructional designer (ID) throughout the design and development process, wherein the ID provides technical, pedagogical, and instructional assistance.

The IDs that assisted the instructors who participated in the debrief sessions have extensive experience designing asynchronous online and blended courses and varying areas of expertise (e.g., more than 3 years working in engineering disciplines). The IDs worked with the instructors for 16–18 weeks, conducting needs analysis on the pedagogical and technological aspects of the course, consulting on research-based approaches for active learning, assisting instructors in the use of audio/video software applications, and advising on instructional choices at each step of the design process.

In a typical new development course project, the workflow includes a needs assessment, alignment of course outcomes to activities and assessments, consolidation of the course structure, regular meetings, content sequencing, assessment design, material development, and course site design. The IDs continue to provide the instructors with technical, instructional, and pedagogical assistance throughout the implementation phase.

The design process is grounded in an adapted analyze, design, develop, implement, and evaluate model in combination with backward design (Grant & Wiggins, 2005). Figure 1 shows the course design grant process, which consists of three collaborative and iterative phases: planning, production, and implementation. At the design phase's conclusion and after the course's first implementation, the IDs conduct debriefs with the course instructor(s). The debriefs allow instructors to reflect on their experience designing, developing, and implementing their asynchronous online/blended courses.

CONCEPTUAL FRAMEWORK

Online learning has revolutionized educational practices with new paradigms, pedagogies, and technologies employed to design courses to enhance student learning experiences. Online education provides higher education institutions with a low-cost, flexible way to reach a global audience (Casey, 2008). With the advent and growth of online learning platforms in higher education, it has become critical to understand the role of online instructors in successful online course design. The foremost step in this direction is to closely examine the experiences of online instructors as they design, develop and teach their online courses. An approach to delve into the instructors' experiences is through debriefs.

Debriefing is an accepted practice in health care sciences for teaching and faculty develop-

FIGURE 1

Course Design Grant Process

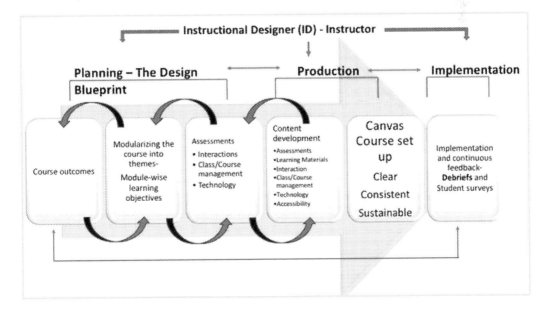

ment (Cheng et al., 2016). It is a discussion and analysis of one's experience through evaluation and exploration of events and experiences (Garderner, 2013). It allows for identifying the areas of improvement and betterment (Garderner, 2013). However, debriefs as a mode to understand the experiences of instructors of higher education asynchronous online courses still need to be discovered. Debriefs, defined in the context of this study as semistructured interviews conducted with the instructors after the first offering of the course, allowed instructors to reflect on their experiences while developing and implementing their online courses. Through debriefs, it is possible to encourage instructors to critically self-reflect on their processes and experiences, revealing their thinking on how the course design process and implementation worked for them.

Reflecting thinking is familiar in educational contexts. In fact, Dewey (1933) was the pioneer in reflective thinking and recognized it as a specialized form of thinking. Dewey's ideas led to the development of Schon's (1983) *reflective practice* and the identification and distinction of *reflection-in-action* (during the experience) and *reflection-on-action* (after the experience) (Schon, 1988). Further, for adults, Mezirow's (1996) transformative learning theory revolutionized our understanding of the way adults thought and experienced learning. In transformative learning theory, "learning is understood as the process of using a prior interpretation to construe a new or revised interpretation of the meaning of one's experience to guide future action" (Mezirow, 1996, p. 162). Furthermore, transformative learning theory "involves transforming frames of reference through a crucial reflection of assumptions, validating contested beliefs through discourse, taking action on one's reflective insight, and critically assessing it" (Mezirow, 1997, p. 11). Two essential aspects of transformative learning are critical self-reflection and critical discourse (Mezirow, 2006). The former encompasses the perspectives acquired through life experiences that enable us to perceive and understand our daily experiences.

Through critical reflection, adults can identify and reevaluate the assumptions on which these perspectives are constructed. Transformative learning theory provides the basis for understanding the instructors' course design undertakings after the fact. Therefore, to understand the experiences of online instructors as they go through the course design process, it is crucial to examine their reflections and the stories that unfold.

RESEARCH DESIGN

This study followed a multiple-case study approach and examined the debriefs conducted by five instructors. The IDs conducted these debriefs after the first iteration of their online course. These cases allowed for a comparison of the experiences of instructors in designing and teaching their asynchronous online courses in different colleges within the university (Yin, 2009).

DATA COLLECTION AND ANALYSIS

The course instructors who participated in the study were from the COE and liberal arts and sciences. They mainly were novice online instructors with no prior asynchronous online teaching experience except for one of the instructors who had a year of online teaching experience. The course these instructors taught were offered in the semesters of fall 2015– spring 2016. All grant-recipients novice online instructors were invited to participate in this study by their assigned instructional designers. They were informed of the study's goals, and participation was voluntary. Five of the instructors responded with their consent for developing their courses. This study followed all the requirements of the university's human subject protection office. Pseudonyms are used to protect the identity of the participants and maintain their anonymity. Table 1 provides the profile of the instructors interviewed.

Ethnographic-style semistructured debriefs were conducted with these instructors, where

What the Debriefs Unfold

29

TABLE 1

Instructors' Teaching Profile

Instructor	Age	Rank/College	Experience Teaching	Prior Asynchronous Online Experience (Years)
Walter	40–50	Associate professor/COE	20+ years	0
Aron	50–60	Professor/COE	20+years	0
Dana	50–60	Associate teaching professor/LAS	8+ years	1
Hannah	40–50	Associate teaching professor/LAS	8+ years	0
Alex	35–40	Associate teaching professor/LAS	8+ years	0

the four stages of ethnographic interview protocol were followed: apprehension, exploration, cooperation, and participation (Spradley, 1979).

As the instructors reflected on their experiences designing and teaching their online courses, it was necessary not to impose any strict structure that would impede their thought process. At the same time, probing or follow-up questions were asked at stages where more clarification or detailed response was needed. These probing questions were asked mainly under four categories (a) experiences with asynchronous online course design, development, and teaching of the course; (b) strengths and weaknesses of the course; (c) experience of working with an ID; and (d) potential course improvements for future offerings.

The interviews took place in each faculty member's office, lasted approximately 45 minutes to an hour and were audio recorded. The debriefs were conducted by IDs not initially assigned to work on the course design project with the instructor(s) to avoid any potential conflict or bias in their responses.

The three researchers involved in this study transcribed and analyzed the audio recordings. Each researcher read a transcription in its entirety to develop a sense of the data. Subsequently, the research team met to code one random transcription together line by line. As they coded, they added keywords and phrases that captured relevant initial ideas of the data.

After that, the three researchers met to discuss each of the five analyzed transcripts. They

discussed the preliminary codes and resolved any discrepancies. After reviewing all five transcripts, these were revised and open-coded, and a preliminary codebook was developed. The within-case analysis allowed the researcher to become more familiar with the cases. Using a preliminary code book, the researchers coded the transcripts individually again and met in pairs to review those. Through a peer-reviewing phase, the researchers reviewed each transcript and updated the codebook. Any disagreements were discussed, and the researchers resolved them by discussing and reaching a consensus (Brinkmann & Kvale, 2015). Adjustments were made, new themes were added if needed, and a consensus was reached for a final code book. Using the final version of the code book, researchers coded the five transcripts for the last time and compared them; the interrater reliability of more than 85% was established, and the emerging themes were finalized. Figure 2 presents the stages of the data analysis cycle.

FINDINGS

The findings revealed that each instructor had a unique design journey. However, by cross-analyzing the ethnographic interviews, some common categories emerged: (a) teaching philosophy, (b) instructor's learning during the design and development process, (c) online experience during implementation of the course, (d) instructor's perception of online learning benefits, (e) instructor's challenges during course designing and during the implementation phase, (f) support from an instructional designer, (g) course improvements, and (h) instructor's content development experience. The frequencies of each code occurring in the transcripts were also calculated.

After considering the frequencies of each code and thoroughly cross-examining the categories across the cases along with relevant evidence from the transcripts, two main themes emerged (a) the evolution of the instructor's understanding of an asynchronous online course: content planning and interactions, (b) the working with an instructional designer (Table 2). These themes, along with the categories associated with them, are detailed next.

EVOLUTION OF INSTRUCTOR'S UNDERSTANDING OF AN ASYNCHRONOUS ONLINE COURSE: CONTENT PLANNING AND INTERACTIONS

All instructors indicated that they had online teaching experience. Their understanding of the asynchronous online course and its design process evolved throughout the varied design phases and the delivery of the courses. In particular, instructors recounted their experience

FIGURE 2

Cycle for Data Analysis

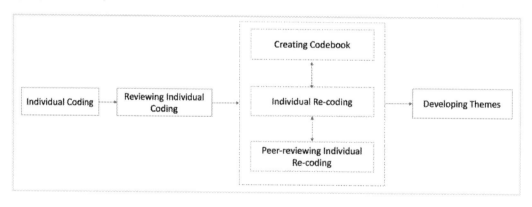

TABLE 2

Categories and Themes That Emerged From the Cross-Analysis of Interviews

Categories	Themes
1. Teaching approach 2. Instructor's learning 3. Learning through online teaching experience 4. Instructor's perceptions of online learning benefits 5. Instructor's challenges during the design and delivery of the course	• Evolution of instructor's understanding of an asynchronous online course: Content planning and interactions
6. Support from an instructional designer 7. Course improvements 7. Instructor's content development experience.	• Working with an instructional designer

as designers of the courses by reflecting on their teaching approach, learning during the design and development stages, online teaching, perceptions of online learning benefits, and challenges during the design and delivery of the course.

Teaching Approach

While reflecting on and describing their experience designing the course, some instructors briefly mentioned their approach to teaching. Some instructors placed greater value on student interaction, while others mentioned the required skills for learning the content and the mechanisms used to distribute the workload for assignments. For example, Hannah said, "Programming is a lot like learning a language. You need to activate the vocabulary, and that's what we were trying to do." Additionally, she compared the timeline for homework between the online and the face-to-face formats, saying that she was used to "giving [students] homework assignments on, say, Tuesday and to the next Tuesday. One week really doesn't work for online students because they usually have a weekend or the nights to work on."

Some instructors who were accustomed to teaching face to face had a perception that in-person interaction between instructor-student and student-student in face-to-face settings would be absent in online teaching. For example, Alex said, "My overall perception was not particularly positive. The in-person interaction with the students, the opportunity for the students to interact with each other in the sort of larger social group, the reinforcement that came from being in the same place at the same time would be missing in online teaching."

In addition, some instructors were accustomed to teaching face to face and were reluctant and conservative to adjust their teaching style. However, the fact that offering their course online would create an opportunity for those students who otherwise would not be enrolled in their course if the course was offered face to face helped some of the instructors decide to teach online. According to Alex,

"I decided to offer our course in summer, entirely online, is that the student body that would attract would be people who might want to take this course and take it to face to face, but for some reason or another couldn't fit into their schedules or some sort of extra commitment."

Learning During the Design and Development Phases

Instructors recognized the importance of the learning outcomes in designing the learning activities and assessments. However, making this alignment explicit and clear through specific word choices in the description of assignments came as a revelation. For example, Dana commented "I had never worked so carefully with the language choices and the Bloom's Taxonomy in terms of, "Okay, here's the learning objective, here's the assignment, and here's how that assignment fulfills that learning objective." I had been doing that, but I never thought about the writing process to make sure that that happened."

Similarly, preparing the online course outline helped create its structure and associated components for Hannah. She commented, "Setting the content and the objectives are most equivalent to the deliverables and the timeline. That helped a lot. That was my skeleton, and that helped me fill in the content pieces." According to Alex, the explicit connection between the different levels of course design was something that he learned and was planning to incorporate going forward. In his words, "How each course outcome connects with an objective in particular modules, the work that is done with particular assessment is very helpful." He also felt that this alignment exercise helped students understand the purpose of the assignment, presenting clearly why they were doing what they were doing in the course.

While digital tools usually aid in delivering content, instructors commented that during their online course development, they learned to use tools more often and more intentionally.

In Dana's case, it never occurred to her that creating lecture notes in PowerPoints and recording them would be an option to replace her weekly text-based notes for students. She said, "This time I used a lot more, made better use of the technology available. Previously, I had typed up lecture notes that students had to read versus recording them with PowerPoints. That was all new, and I think that was more effective."

Likewise, Hannah shared her positive experience creating the lecture recording by writing transcripts and using the Camtasia video recording software. She said, "Assembling the slide deck and then writing a transcript for every single slide worked for me. Once I had the transcript, I noticed that some things were easier to talk about and some things needed a little bit of fine-tuning." She also mentioned that she eventually got used to using Camtasia software to record videos and felt more adventurous. She said, "By the end, I was a bit more adventurous, and I did some freestyle. Sometimes I was showing students hands-on software. At that point, I was really recording myself doing what I wanted them to see and talking about it, so I also talk out loud. Experience for them so they could follow along what I was doing. They also hear the thoughts."

In addition, instructors' understanding of what an online course encompasses was limited to equating it to delivering recorded lectures. In this format, a live face-to-face class was recorded and distributed to distance students, who would log in to the class synchronously or view the recorded materials later. A learning management system (LMS) was used primarily as a repository for lecture notes and the delivery of recorded materials. Learning to design their online course was, the reflection words of Mark, "a rather dramatic change in the way I teach my course." Another example of an instructor's understanding of the nature of an online course can be illustrated in Hannah's comment: "I've taught some online courses. One thing that we sometimes do is to just tape a class while it's happening. I always feel bad for those students who have to watch those tapes, because it's about something that they just observe, and they don't participate in it."

Similarly, Aron mentioned,

> I did teach ELO courses in past, but just did captures or face to face lectures, so when I actually was doing face to face lecture and have students in front of me, so I felt I was talking to other students. But when I was doing recording, just talking to the computer, it was a different experience but in general it was good.

All instructors acknowledged that there was an initial intense time investment in the content planning phase. This phase included creating observable and measurable course learning outcomes, modularizing and making the content more concrete, sequencing the content in meaningful and coherent modules, and detailing assignment instructions previously verbally presented in the face-to-face course. Instructors also acknowledged that the time invested in such content planning processes intensified in comparison to the planning phase of a face-to-face class. For example, Aron shared, "It was generally a good experience, although it took longer time than expected for preparation and trying to perfect the lectures and so on." Similarly, Hannah felt surprised that planning to develop an online course involved a *heavily front-loaded* process. She said,

> What basically happened was that for each movie that I made, I spend about 10 hours assembling the material and making all the slides, doing the voiceover, piecing everything together as a movie. About an hour for each minute is about a fair assessment of what I needed in terms of time.

In addition to spending more time on content creation for their online courses, the instructors mentioned that most of their time was also spent on grading assessments. Alex spent the "vast majority of time grading the assessments, reading what students had written and giving the feedback to their discussion posts."

Learning Through Online Teaching Experience

Understating interactions, student-student, and student-teacher in an asynchronous online course was a learning experience for the instructors. With their prior face-to-face experience, interactions mainly consisted of in-class questions by students, immediate intervention by the instructor if needed, or another in-class communication. For course updates, the instructors would verbally announce them in class. Instructors relied on verbal and visual cues while delivering their lectures and paced the content covered in class or provided remedial lectures. However, in the asynchronous online environments, the absence of such interactions and immediate feedback made the instructors reflect on adjusting their teaching strategies, assessments, instructions, and support the workload students would do. Some comments relate to, "how to pace the lecture, that part is different, in the in-classroom lectures, I could have interactions with the students and then I can adjust the pace adaptively, If I know that students are not getting it, then I can stop it and slow down, gave more hindsight."

According to Alex teaching online helped him think about how assessments can be redesigned in a way that the students have a clear sense of what is expected from them. In his words, "The biggest thing I learnt and need to do is have a clearer design of rubrics for the assessments in advance and to direct the students to it early, and often."

Dana, in turn, compares the work and emphasis placed on a face-to-face and an online class. She mentioned the workload in a face-to-face class "you can't do in an online class. I think that's partly because, during class time, we do a lot of the work, and online it's more students driven in terms of when they do it."

The instructors critically examined the nature of interactions in an online class. For these instructors, interactions were redefined according to the affordances of the LMS or the online meeting applications, such as Zoom. Instructors' understanding of the nature of an online asynchronous space evolved from being apprehensive of the type and quality of interaction to valuing the various channels by which interaction was facilitated along with the frequency and quality of communication. In their respective courses, instructors also had online office hours at scheduled times and days where students could come and interact with the instructor synchronously. Instructors heavily employed graded and nongraded discussion forums to facilitate interaction. According to the instructors, such platforms promoted student-student engagement in the online space. For example, Aaron commented, "The discussion forums, in fact, supplemented the completely asynchronous teaching mode by having students actually engage in the discussions and so on." The discussion boards were also seen to promote cognitive presence and engagement. Aaron also mentioned, "I think the discussion forums were actually very good rather than just talk to the computer, the students watching the videos and so on, so engaging them in the discussion through the discussion forum, this was actually very helpful."

Nevertheless, the asynchronous nature of the discussion forums posed challenges to instructors to intervene timely when the topic of the discussions was drifting from its focus and bringing superficiality to the posts. For example, Dana pointed out that,

> in the online version, since students were doing things at different times, there was sometimes, some disagreement on concepts and it was happening, which a lot of students posted at 3:00 am, I wasn't monitoring it, so I couldn't intervene and make a correction.... Then, once I did add my thoughts in, I don't know if the students actually even came back and read it.

Hannah, in turn, mentioned that she had thought that the depth of the discussions would involve critical thinking as exhibited in the face-to-face class; instead, the discussions "didn't quite work out. The discussions were much more shallow. [Students] didn't seem to really get into the material. There were a lot of preconceived notions, and they kept repeating those preconceived notions."

The instructors compiled any critical information shared in the discussion forums or via emails and shared it with the class using the Announcements tool in the LMS. This process of communicating further evolved instructors' understanding of how critical their presence was for keeping a regular stream of communication with their students. By communicating with students often, instructors could also reflect on the course continuously. This is illustrated in Walter's comment, "Also, they interact among themselves online, and that's good because if one student has a question, then others can help him or her."

Whereas Hannah mentioned that in her class, the interaction with students mainly took place via the announcements tool in the LMS. She said,

> I use the announcement tools to make regular announcements. Whenever there were two, three questions that I had got from students via email, I would collect all of those and just give them an update or remind them of their lines or try to clarify something on the syllabus that wasn't quite clear. Usually, my announcement has three or four points. It was mostly me checking in with them.

Perceptions of Online Learning Benefits

For some instructors, it was evident that the online format benefits the students and instructors alike. These advantages ranged from the flexible timeline of assignment submissions to connecting concepts to application exercises. For students in Hannah's statistic class to demonstrate they could program and resolve questions, the quizzes were flexible. The online quizzes facilitated a two-way approach,

checking for understanding through an active task that could be done unlimited times. Hannah described the quizzing approach as follows,

> we had something that we called *fast finger programming*. We would give [students] a dataset ahead of time and say, "The maximum yield that year was ..." Then out of a set of questions, [students] had to pick the maximum which means that on the side, they had to have the program open and determine quickly within two minutes how they could get the quantity. Then in the response report, the little piece of code that they could use to get that quantity. They have to actively put something in rather than us asking them passively.get points if they repeat ... they could do [students] them in unlimited number of times. They would, for sure, get the points out and if they have to redo it 10 times, so be it. It was a set of usually 20 questions or so, and they had to do five [randomly selected].

For other instructors, the online course offered students a feasible learning option when they could not enroll in a face-to-face class. According to Alex, "The online format is an opportunity to bring the material to people who want it, who are interested in it, but who can't otherwise get to it."

CHALLENGES DURING THE COURSE DESIGN AND DELIVERY PHASES

All instructors reported challenges in the design and delivery stages of the online course. These challenges included an increased workload, a reconceptualization of the course structure, a change of mindset, and using digital tools. Despite some instructors' prior online teaching experience, there was a steep learning curve as they engaged in a structured yet flexible design process. The learning curve for Dana involved designing the course in weekly modules to provide more consistency to the content and to get used to the pace of students' work each week. As she pointed out,

What the Debriefs Unfold 35

With the module method, we opened the module on a Sunday, and the students had seven days to complete all the work for that module. Where in my face-to-face classes, I'm used to saying, "Okay, this is due on Friday... I had to get accustomed to students working at different paces. There were certain students who would do everything on Sunday and others that would submit things at the least minute on Saturday. It was just sort of a different mindset in terms of things continually coming in versus all at once.

Teaching the online course required instructors to set a plan for monitoring students' participation and grading assignments. While the face-to-face class had a structured weekly schedule when students came to class and submitted assignments, the online format, while giving students broader flexibility to complete their coursework, required that instructors set a plan for the workload. Dana commented that "I felt like I had to be much more committed to checking email, and checking in with the class, because there wasn't that face-to-face instruction, but also because students worked at their different paces."

Whereas for Alex, grading, while providing effective and helpful feedback, was his biggest challenge. For him providing feedback different than the assessment instruction was a challenge. In his words,

If they just didn't do it, or what they did seemed to suggest they clearly didn't understand what it was that was being asked of them, that is a greater challenge, because that requires me to figure out what kind of comments, what kind of feedback I can give back such that when they attempt to do it the next time that they will do it better. How to make that feedback sound different from the instructions that I gave them at the front end.

The instructors were amazed at the workload required to develop their online courses. Hannah shared that

What was really a surprise to me was how heavily front-loaded online courses are. In retrospect, I should have started earlier. I did

start sometime in May. At that point, my summer was booked with conferences and travel. I just didn't have a lot of time or not enough time to prepare all of the online materials.

Aron said,

the main challenges actually were, first the deadlines. For example, I know I had to post the lectures online at a certain time and other issue was that specially at the very beginning to prepare a lecture, it took a long time, for example I had to record them and edit trying to perfect the lecture.

Instructors also faced challenges in adjusting to grading in the online environment. For Dana, providing feedback felt "less personal since I was clicking buttons versus writing much feedback." Dana relied heavily on rubrics and could write less feedback than she was used to in the face-to-face class.

The second major theme that emerged from the analysis of the debriefs was the working relationship between the instructor and the ID. Specifically, instructors described their experience in terms of the support from an ID while also discussing their content development experience and future course improvements.

SUPPORT FROM AN INSTRUCTIONAL DESIGNER

Instructors recognized the value of collaborative work with their IDs. They expressed their appreciation for the guidance received regarding content sequencing, that is, the length of each module, the pacing of the different assignments, and the type and format of assignments. They also received guidance on creating their syllabus and schedule and LMS design, including course structure, layout, visual elements, and navigation. Aaron described the suggestions he received and how important those were, including different methods of assessment, especially discussion forums. For him, "[discussion boards] played a pivotal role in getting the online students involved because, without these discussion forums that you have suggested, I think that the interaction with online students would have been to a much lesser degree."

According to the instructors, their IDs helped with project management tasks, facilitating advancement in the course design in a timely manner. Some comments that support these findings include the following:

Also, follow up on the deadlines, also the email messages that [ID] used to send us. Actually, this kind of puts some kind of pressure actually, not in a bad way pressure on us to pay more attention to recording the lectures and putting the material online. Otherwise, things may have dragged a little bit, yeah ... the responsiveness is excellent and very helpful. I never could have done this without the help that I got ... I liked that the ID, at least, seemed to have a plan. I don't have a plan going in. The ID worked with me with weekly deadlines. Chunking up the material helped me design the course."

Some of the instructors reflected on the evolution of their partnership with their IDs. These instructors recognized that the relationship was collaborative toward a common goal where they worked as a team,

I think [ID] and I had a great working relationship. She presented ideas. She was very efficient in terms of, here's our agenda for what we're going to talk about, by the next time we meet, here are some of the things you're going to accomplish, here's the thing I'm going to accomplish... I felt like it was a really great collaborative process. (Dana)

Additionally, instructors valued the knowledge and pedagogical expertise that their IDs brought to the projects. The ID lens helped the instructors take up some challenges to reconsider their approach to content coverage and workload. As Dana highlighted in the interview,

When she pushed me from changing this course calendar from dates to modules, like, kudos to her for doing that ... because it

made life a lot easier ... because of her experience, [she] could look at it and say, "You're making a lot of work for yourself." And I couldn't see it at the time, but with her experience she would jump in and say, "Oh, you need to streamline, or cut, or something," so that was really helpful.

Alex mentioned that the guidance he received from an ID on converting a large-scale face-to-face 16-week course with substantial content to an 8-week summer online course was invaluable. In his words, "The sense of what was appropriate amount of material to assign from week to week in terms of reading and assessments. What are the kinds of online resources, clear instructions, clear rubrics is the kind of feedback of help received from ID and was absolutely essential, and made the course successful as it was, I feel."

One salient challenge that instructors faced was identifying ways to involve students in the online environment. Working with IDs helped instructors overcome this challenge by following best practices and alternative assessment ideas. Aron appreciated ID's help identifying alternative assessments for his course, which helped in student involvement. In his words,

ID proposed four different methods of assessments, actually discussion forums; in fact, I think they played a pivotal role in getting the online students involved because without these discussion forums that ID had suggested, I think that the interaction with online students would have been to a much lesser degree.

FUTURE COURSE IMPROVEMENTS

The design and teaching of the online course allowed instructors to reflect on their experience and use the challenges faced as catalysts for improvements. The redevelopment activities ranged from visual design and iconography to the length of the course and workload for students and instructors. In Dana's discussion-based class, the improvements related to reducing the seats open for the course and the length of the lecture videos. The class involved a heavy load of reading and writing required for students to participate in the discussions actively, and Dana pointed out that "for 40 students, I couldn't write the feedback that I'm used to in the face-to-face class… and do that in a timely manner." In addition, she planned to shorten the lectures to less than 16 minutes.

CONTENT DEVELOPMENT EXPERIENCE

The content development experience explicitly related to the process from planning to creating the learning materials, activities, and assessments. For example, structuring the course into coherent and logical modules, creating a detailed course schedule for the whole course with precise due dates for all deliverables, and sequencing the content, were some of the most common comments in the debrief interviews. Aligning assignments to outcomes and clearly describing their purposes and instructions was critical for the online class. Dana explained that she had to describe the assignments in more detail for students to understand the expectations. She had to "think about the way in which the instructions were written for assignments and write out everything I would normally supplement with verbal instructions…. Okay, when I've given this assignment before, what were the questions students asked?' to try to be more proactive with that as I wrote the assignments."

Also, planning, shortening, and recording lectures were challenging and gave the instructors a new perspective on structuring and planning the content. Walter commented "breaking the lecture into smaller parts. This was actually difficult for me to understand the students would like to see 15 minutes or 20 minutes maximum lecture."

The development of the lectures was a "time-consuming" process that involved most of the instructors in learning how to record, pace, and edit the video recordings themselves.

However, developing the content was regarded as a good learning experience.

DISCUSSION

This paper examined instructors' experiences developing their online courses through debriefs. The two main themes that emerged from the data included (a) the evolution of the instructor's understanding of an asynchronous online course and (b) working with an instructional designer. These themes encapsulate several concepts that illustrate the experience of instructors designing their first online courses (refer to Table 2 for details of these concepts and themes). These two themes will be discussed in detail in the following sections.

Evolution of Instructor's Understanding of an Asynchronous Online Course

While the instructors in this study recognized the importance and relevance of the course learning outcomes, it needed to be clarified how to use the outcomes as a guide to design the learning activities and assessments. During the development process, instructors aligned the content and assignments they created to the course outcomes. In other words, the instructors used the learning outcomes as starting points to identify how students would be able to demonstrate their learning (Biggs & Tang, 2011). The instructors also relied on the outcomes to design transparent assessments with clear deliverables, time lines, and instructions. Instructors further reflected on how the outcomes facilitated restructuring the content into more manageable pieces and helped them in the intentional use of digital tools. Instructors entered into a discovery stage with several revelations to develop an understanding that in order to develop their online course, it was paramount to adopt a student-centered strategy guided by the outcomes.

Considering that the instructors in this study had vast face-to-face teaching experience, the online learning environment challenged them to step out of their teaching comfort zone. At the beginning of the design projects, these instructors needed help to envision interactive online communication with students. For most of these instructors, not seeing the students and their interactions prompted them to consider that the online space would isolate students and would prevent them from a robust and engaging exchange of ideas, a common concern many instructors have about online learning (Boulos et al., 2005; Comer & Lenaghan, 2013).

Furthermore, instructors feared that the online space would prevent them from communicating with students efficiently; delivering the instructions and course information verbally. Unbeknownst to instructors, they were concerned with their online *presence* in the course; however, this presence was narrowly believed to be similar to being present physically in the face-to-face class. The instructors were concerned about conveying a sense of presence in an environment where participants do not see each other in real time. Thus, instructors were evolving in their understanding that their *presence* would involve more than being there; it would include using different means and tools to guide the students' learning experience (Kelly, 2014)

Despite instructors' plans to utilize several methods to interact with students, including announcements and discussion boards, these instructors wondered if communicating with students, as they usually did face to face, would be possible online. However, during the delivery of their courses, the instructors realized that *being present* in the online environment was not only possible but that interaction in the online space goes beyond giving instructions on assignments or promoting student-to-student interaction. Instructors became aware of the affordances of the online environment to allow for different types and formats of interaction, ranging from scheduled office hours, more intentional feedback on assignments, the use of announcements, and nongraded discussion boards.

Along with the topic of interaction, instructors realized that their presence understood as the instructor being there or making them "visible and real" to students, was one critical aspect of their online teaching (Kelly, 2014). Nevertheless, the asynchronous nature of the courses posed an additional challenge to instructors timely intervention. Some of the instructors raised concerns about needing help to monitor students' contributions in the discussions and intervene timely if needed. These instructors could have realized that the online environment's asynchronicity gives the advantage of carefully responding to the posts and enhancing the quality of the interactions (Rovai, 2007).

Working With an Instructional Designer

Instructors in this study worked closely with an instructional designer throughout the online courses' design, development, and delivery. While working with their IDs, the instructors realized that designing their online course would demand substantial time and continuous pedagogical adaptations to meet the goals, of course, design quality (Burdett, 2003). The content preparation workload for the instructors in this study increased substantially during the design and development stages. The intensity and time necessary for creating the course plan and learning activities were unexpected by all instructors.

The front-loaded process that the instructors followed required them to plan a course blueprint that would showcase a modular (e.g., weekly, unit, chapter) content structure organized cohesively and aligned to the outcomes. While instructors should have completed the development of all the content, including activities and assignments, prior to delivering the course, some course developments happened while the courses were in progress. This impacted even further the time commitment and availability of instructors to create the content and learning materials in the LMS in a timely manner, with some instructors needing to be a week ahead of students' completion of the previous weekly module. Considering that a practical approach to the quality of the course design is to have a consistent structure and, thus, the learning experience (Rottmann & Rabidoux, 2017), instructors realized that they needed to also plan for the course delivery. This plan involved ensuring that all content modules had a consistent structure and organization, strategizing the instructors' participation in the discussion boards, and establishing a time frame for grading assignments.

In addition, instructors placed greater value and praise on the collaborative and supportive demeanor of their ID for the successful development of the course. According to the instructors, the assistance from the IDs exceeded the course design process. Instructors acknowledged that IDs facilitated project management tasks, including keeping pace with the time lines, and balanced the workload for developing and delivering the course.

A remarkable aspect of the ID's support is that instructors view it as a collaborative endeavor. This collaboration allowed IDs to guide instructors in the course development project through their pedagogical, technological, and learning theories expertise. In contrast, instructors trusted the instructional design choices regarding course design and delivery. Instructors viewed these collaborations as an important part of their support system.

However, instructors appeared to have been challenged during the conversations with their IDs, becoming aware of the reasons for the instructional design decisions (e.g., breaking down the content into manageable pieces and creating rubrics). This was captured within a conducive environment that allowed IDs to challenge misconceptions of instructors about online teaching and learning and for instructors to move from their instructional/teaching comfort zones. The collaborative experience that instructors had with their IDs underscores the recognition that to function as an effective team member, it is critical to value the different talents that each other brings into the course development projects, facilitated

through active listening and trust (Richardson et al., 2018), and to meet instructors where they are in their online pedagogy.

CONCLUSIONS

This multicase study highlighted the experiences of an instructor through the design and development process of their asynchronous online course. The findings presented how the instructor's beliefs related to online learning and teaching evolved during the design phases of their courses as they worked with an ID, particularly their understanding of an online course, the work and time commitments needed to design one, course interactions, content planning, and sequencing. The findings also showcased the value IDs bring with their pedagogical and technical skills and project management strategies. These debriefs go beyond making the experiences and reflections visible. However, they also represent a step toward making the instructor a reflective practitioner, which is seen as a combination of self-awareness, reflection, and critical thinking (Eby, 2001).

The instructors in this study had the opportunity to list the ways to better their course for an enhanced learning experience. In contrast, IDs identified the areas where instructors could be better supported throughout the design and development endeavor. Conducting debriefs after the design process can be a critical tool for the instructors to reflect on their design process and teaching adaptations for online environments. It is also an insightful tool for IDs to improve their approach to pedagogical and technological assistance. A better understanding of processes and philosophies for the instructor and the IDs can lead to more effective course design collaborative practices and potentially better learner experiences.

LIMITATIONS AND FUTURE STUDY

This multiple-case study was conducted in a particular university setting within an online learning unit that awarded a grant for funding the design and development of online courses with the support of an ID. While the study provides deep insights into faculty experiences, the findings should be cautiously applied to other educational contexts with a different culture and support system.

This study can be extended to examine how such reflections enhance the design process and lead to better asynchronous online courses. Conducting further debriefs with instructors experienced in asynchronous online teaching can provide a better understanding of their instructional decisions to enhance students' learning, communication, and types of presence. The study presented here could be further extended to be included as one critical step in any instructional design model.

REFERENCES

Boud, D., Keogh, R., & Walker, D. (2013). *Reflection: Turning experience into learning.* Routledge.

Allen, I.E., & Seaman, J. (with R. Poulin & T. T. Straut). (2016). *Online report card: Tracking online education in the United States.* Babson Survey Research Group. http://www.onlinelearningsurvey.com/highered.html

Baldwin, S. J., Ching, Y. H., & Friesen, N. (2018). Online course design and development among college and university instructors: An analysis using grounded theory. *Online Learning, 22*(2), 157–171. https://doi.org/10.24059/olj.v22i2.121

Baran, E., Correia, A.-P., & Thompson, A. (2011). Transforming online teaching practice: Critical analysis of the literature on the roles and competencies of online teachers. *Distance Education, 32*(3), 421–439. https://doi.org/10.1080/01587919.2011.610293

Cheng, A., Morse, K. J., Rudolph, J., Arab, A. A., Runnacles, J., & Eppich, W. (2016). Learner-centered debriefing for health care simulation education: Lessons for faculty

development. *Simulation in Healthcare, 11*(1), 32–40.

Clandinin, D. J., & Connelly, F. M. (Eds.). (1995). *Teachers' professional knowledge landscapes.* Teachers College Press.

Dewey, J. (1933). *How we think: A restatement of the relation of reflective thinking to the educative process.* Henry Regnery.

Dhawan, S. (2020). Online learning: A panacea in the time of COVID-19 crisis. *Journal of Educational Technology Systems, 49*(1), 5–22.

Eby, M. A. (2000). Understanding professional development. In A. Brechin, H. Brown, & M. A. Eby (Eds.), *Critical practice in health and social care* (pp. 113–142). SAGE.

Fook, J. (2006) Beyond reflective practice: reworking the "critical" in critical reflection. Keynote speech for the conference "Professional lifelong learning: Beyond reflective practice." *Reflective Practice, 1*(2), 183–198.

Gardner, R. (2013, June). Introduction to debriefing. *Seminars in Perinatology, 37*(3), 166–174.

Heuer, B. P., & King, K. P. (2004). Leading the band: The role of the instructor in online learning for educators. *The Journal of Interactive Online Learning, 3*(1), 1–11.

Jaggars, S. S., & Xu, D. (2016). How do online course design features influence student performance? Computers & Education, 95, 270–284.

Larrivee, B. (2000). Transforming teaching practice: Becoming the critically reflective teacher. *Reflective Practice, 1*(3), 293–307.

Mezirow, J. (1997). Transformative learning: Theory to practice. *New Directions for Adult and Continuing Education, 74,* 5–12.

Misra, P. K., & Chauhan, P. S. (2020). Online teaching and learning experiences during COVID-19 lockdowns: Ten lessons for higher education institutions. *University News, 58,* 31.

Newton, J. M. (2000). Uncovering knowing in practice amongst a group of undergraduate student nurses. *Reflective Prac-*

tice, 1(2), 183–197. https://doi.org/ 10.1080/713693152

Spradley, J. (1979). *The ethnographic interview*. Holt, Rinehart, & Winston.

Taylor, E. W. (2008). Transformative learning theory. *New Directions for Adult and Continuing Education, 119,* 5–15. https://doi.org/10.1002/ace.301

Yin, R. (2009). *Case study research: Design and methods.* SAGE.

THE URBANIZATION
OF DISTANCE EDUCATION IN AUSTRALIA

Chris Radcliffe
School of Dentistry and Medical Sciences, Charles Sturt University, Orange, Australia

This article explores the changing nature of P–12 distance education, from its traditional roots of rural and remote students to urban students seeking an alternative to conventional school. The present study examined distance education in the Australian context, focusing on Queensland, through a semistructured survey of parents ($n = 43$) across three distance education schools. This study explored the child's learning location, context, and academic and social engagement as determined by the parent. In addition, this study examined the reasons why parents selected distance education over a conventional day school. Findings from this study indicated a high uptake of distance education by families residing in large regional and urban settings. This data contrasts the traditional roots and the common understanding of distance education in Australia. This article further explores factors contributing to the growth of distance education. It presents current and future trends that may respond to distance education students' changed demographics and learning needs.

Originally termed *external studies* and later known as *correspondence learning*, distance education in Queensland has experienced significant growth in recent years (Independent Schools Queensland, 2021). Distance education in Australia, was initiated in 1909 at the secondary school level and then in 1914 at the primary school level when state governments were mandated to provide an education program to all children (Reiach et al., 2012; Stacey, 2005). Such was the success of correspondence education that "Australia can claim to be the first country to have shown in a systematic way and on a large scale, that it is possible to provide, by correspondence, a complete elementary education for children who have never been to school" (Cunningham, 1931, p. 9).

While the term distance education is broad, the Department of Education in New South Wales defines distance education as "an equity program for … students who are geographically isolated or whose circumstances prevent them from regularly attending school" (https://education.nsw.gov.au/).

The recent pandemic found teachers nationwide reliant on the technologies that distance education was already well versed. Technology

---

• **Correspondence concerning this article should be addressed to:** Chris Radcliffe, radcliffechris@hotmail.com

The Quarterly Review of Distance Education, Volume 24(1), 2023, pp. 43–54
Copyright © 2023 Information Age Publishing, Inc.

ISSN 1528-3518
All rights of reproduction in any form reserved.

and distance education have a historical narrative of being synonymous, with education providers taking a front-foot approach to implementing technology for improved educational outcomes. Correspondence education initiated the two-way radio, opening the way for direct access to teaching and learning, which had previously only been achieved through curriculum received via the postal service. Providers of correspondence education were quick to adapt new technologies such as audio and later video tape recorders and then establish an audio graphic network that linked modems and allowed for shared screens, enabling collaborative sharing of a teacher (Stacey, 2005).

From the humble beginnings of correspondence education, distance education has continued to flourish (Reiach et al., 2012), and distance education providers have been quick to adopt new and emerging technologies, including online ecosystems such as the Google Classroom, Blackboard, Canvas, and other platforms, creating a space for explicit teaching and a rigorous and responsive curriculum. In terms of learning outcomes, distance education in online learning is at least as effective as conventional education and often more effective (Hannum et al., 2008).

THE CURRENT POSITION OF DISTANCE EDUCATION IN AUSTRALIA

There are various independent and public distance education providers across Australia. New South Wales offers the greatest options for distance education providers ($n = 18$), followed by Queensland ($n = 12$) and then the Northern Territory ($n = 3$), see Table 1. Distance education sector enrollments have increased over the past 5 years; in fact, Queensland has seen a 52% increase in enrollments in independent distance education over the past 5 years (Independent Schools Queensland, 2021). Recent enrollment growth has been, in part, the result of the recent global pandemic, growing by 12.5%. However, growth in distance education preceded the pandemic (Independent Schools Queensland, 2021).

TEACHING AND LEARNING IN DISTANCE EDUCATION

A range of terms are used to describe the learning program of a child working from home, including distance education, flexible education, home study, home education, remote learning, online learning, external learning, and at-home learning (Bozkurt, 2019) and each of these terms has discretely different pedagogical approaches. While the pedagogical approach to distance education will vary from school to school, the following section broadly outlines some of the considerations which distance education providers may consider when designing an appropriate pedagogical framework.

Asynchronous and Synchronous

Distance education pedagogy may be broadly divided into two critical modes of learning: synchronous and asynchronous. Asynchronous learning is an independent approach whereby a student learns independently or on their computer via a school learning management system (LMS), such as Moodle, Blackboard, and Google Classroom. Asynchronicity offers students a range of benefits, including a broader choice of study options, flexibility, and expediency. It allows a learner to more or less work at their own pace, which may contribute to a greater depth of learning (Serdyukov, 2020). While asynchronous learning allows anywhere and anytime access for students, the lack of immediacy in teacher feedback can slow the learning process (Persada et al., 2022). Distance education which incorporates synchronous learning requires teachers to develop specific skills, including understanding how to use technologies to connect with students, employing strategies to make remote students seem "real," helping students feel comfortable with technology, and designing learning tasks that foster students' inquiry, construction of meaning and deep learning and ability to build community in the online classroom (Rehn et al., 2018).

In contrast to the static nature of asynchronous learning, synchronous learning offers a live and interactive learning environment providing dynamic, collaborative, and immediacy learning, which involves the learner, the teacher/instructor, and other learners (Serdyukov, 2020). Synchronous learning in distance education may include live web conferences and virtual classrooms (He et al., 2020)

Distance education can respond directly to a student's needs, be it synchronous, asynchronous, or, most commonly, a blend of both modes of learning.

The Role of the Parent

Essential to a successful learning program is the provision of a parent.[1] The role of the parent is to supervise the distance education learning program, liaise with their child's teachers, and, during the early learning years in particular, provide one-to-one tutoring. Parents are generally the mothers who are also required to perform home duties alongside their role of a home tutor (Forlin & Tierney, 2006). Thus any pedagogical approach to distance education should acknowledge the diverse roles of the parent.

Direct Instruction

Established around 4 decades ago, direct instruction sought

> efficiency and effectiveness of instruction through program design, organization of instruction, and positive student-teacher interaction. The approach attempts to control all the significant variables that impact student learning through the placement and grouping of students into instructional groups, the rate and type of examples presented by the teacher, the wording that teach-

TABLE 1

Distance Education Providers in Australia

State	Independent Distance Education School	Level	Public Distance Education Schools	Level
Victoria	—	—	1	P–12
New South Wales	1	P–12	2	Preschool
			9	Primary
			6	Secondary
Queensland	5	P–12	4	P–12
	1	P–10	2	P–10
South Australia	—	—	1	P–12
Tasmania	—	—	1	K–10
Western Australia	1	P–12	1	K–12
	1	7–12		
Northern Territory	—	—	1	10–12
			2	P–9
Australian Capital Territory	—	—	1	Primary
			1	Secondary

Sources: Good Schools Guide (2021) and The Northern Territory Government (2021).

ers use to teach specific concepts and skills, the frequency and type of review of material introduced, the assessment of student's mastery of the material covered, and the responses by teachers to students' attempts to learn the material. (Stockard, 2011, p. 3)

While proponents claim direct instruction to be ineffective (see Eppley & Dudley-Marling, 2019), direct instruction within early years and lower primary school distance education may offer the parent a clear and explicit curriculum program that the parent can present to the child.

Flexibility

Anytime anyplace; this theme emerged from an analysis by Veletsianos and Houlden (2019) of flexible learning in distance education. The anytime-anyplace concept was noted as a state "of being in which learning and teaching are increasingly freed from the limitations of the time, place, and pace of study" (Naidu, 2017, p. 269). This sense of freedom allows learners to establish learning routines and processes to fit their learning styles, whether first thing in the morning, late in the evening, on weekends or to fit within their part-time work. Flexible learning has also been identified as vital for youth disenfranchised or disengaged from mainstream school (Riele et al., 2017). Raising the attainment of upper school completion is a national government objective, and the flexibility of distance education may have a more significant role in this than is currently identified.

Research Question/Purpose

This paper seeks to better understand the current context of distance education. The present study asks three questions (a) What is the learning location and context of the child, (b) What were the key motivations for parents in selecting distance education, (c) Are the children who study via distance education engaged in their learning and socially connected?

METHODOLOGY

This small-scale research study included three distance education providers. Research participants were parents of both Primary and Secondary school-aged children (5–18 years) who were enrolled in distance education at the time of the research project. A total of 43 responses were made to the survey across three distance education providers.

This research applied a semistructured survey. The semistructured survey used Google Forms, allowing the dispersion of online surveys. The survey included open and closed questions but mainly comprised of checkbox options, allowing it to be completed quickly and easily. The survey was split into three key areas: (a) the learning location and context, (b) the reasons/motivations for selecting distance education, and (c) the child's educational and social engagement.

The method of data analysis was thematic analysis. Thematic analysis is an inductive approach that identifies and analyses patterns and meaning from data by illustrating themes important within the context of the study (Joffe, 2012). Fereday and Muir-Cochrane (2006, p. 4) describe thematic analysis as "a form of pattern recognition within the data, where emerging themes become the categories for analysis."

RESULTS AND DISCUSSION

Study Context

This study was applied across three medium-sized nonstate Prep to Year 12 distance education schools. At the time of the study, there were approximately 2,600 students enrolled across the three distance education schools. The study was undertaken in the Australian state of Queensland. Queensland is one of six states of Australia and comprises a population size of 5,217,653 people across a land area of 1,701,712 square kilometers (Australian Bureau of Statistics, 2022). The capital city of Queensland is Brisbane, a medium-sized city with a population of 2,568,927 people (Australian Bureau of Statistics, 2022).

Learning Context of Distance Education Students

This section of the paper seeks to understand better the learning context of the students undertaking distance educations.

The semistructured survey requested participants to respond to three key areas of the learner's context: (a) geographical isolation; (b) the primary "at-home tutor"; (c) location of learning.

Geographical Location

From its roots in catering to remote and rurally located students who may not have had access to conventional schooling (such as those on cattle stations), the current demographics of distance education students have significantly shifted. The survey asked respondents to list the postcode of their current residence. Analysis of the survey responses, Table 2, found a high proportion of respondents (49%) were located within 100 km of Brisbane, the capital city of Queensland. Of the respondents located more than 100 km from Brisbane, the majority (67%) resided within the postcodes of large regional towns, resulting in 87% of respondents residing in an urban or large regional setting. Of the postcodes provided by respondents, there were corresponding options of one or more conventional day schools (either state or independent or both). While this is a small-scale data set, it is evident that distance education has shifted from rural and remote learning locations to urban settings.

The shift of the traditional distance education demographics of remote and rural families to families located in an urban or regional center may indicate various changes to the schooling landscape, including a greater acceptance of distance education, changing perceptions of education, and that, with improved educational technologies, distance education looks and feels more like a conventional day school. Distance education providers should consider the changed demographics of their students and ensure that learning programs are relevant to their contexts.

Distance education is defined as "an equity program for … students who are geographically isolated or whose individual circumstances prevent them from regularly attending school" (https://education.nsw.gov.au/), yet with such a shift in the proportion of students who are geographically isolated, a reviewed definition is proposed, being:

> an educational program which is pedagogically designed so as to allow the student and educator to be spatially separate.

The above definition removes the notion that students are geographically isolated and creates a sense of a more equitable education program.

Role of the Parent

According to the enrollment applications of distance education providers, parents who enroll their children in distance education must nominate a home tutor. The role of the home

TABLE 2

Postcode of Respondents in Brisbane

	0–25kms From Brisbane	25–50kms From Brisbane	50–100kms From Brisbane	More Than 100kms From Brisbane
Proportion of respondents	27%	12%	10%	51%

tutor varies; however, typically, the home tutor will facilitate/monitor the child's learning program. The role of the home tutor generally shifts as a child progresses from preparatory to Year 12. In the early learning setting, the home tutor has a more explicit and intentional role with the child, working alongside in a dual role with the distance education teacher, and then, as the child's learning independence grows, the role of the home tutor shifts to that of a coach/mentor role resulting in the distance education teacher being the primary educator. The survey results found that of the $n = 43$ respondents, the home tutor was primarily the role of the mother (93%). As the mother is the nominated home tutor, this limits her capacity to work, leaving most distance education families reliant on a single income, the father's. The inability to dual income may be a key limitation to growth within the distance education sector. Distance education providers may need to consider household income when setting out school fees.

Location of Student Learning

The pedagogical approach of distance education providers is diverse, yet this creates an opportunity for parents to seek a learning program that aligns with family needs and geographical location. For example, more rural-based families may seek the paper-based learning program due to constraints concerning their internet service, and another family may seek the online program if their child learns and engages well within the online platforms. The location of learning for students studying distance education was overwhelmingly the home ($n = 41$), with only $n = 2$ families nominating a library as the main learning area and $n = 1$ undertaking learning within a workplace. Understanding the location of learning may guide the pedagogical framework of the various distance education providers; for example, knowing that the majority of learners are located in the home may enable providers to undertake teacher/teacher aide visits to the home in order to support both the child and the home tutor.

Motivation for Learning Through Distance Education

This paper sought to understand better the motivations for parents electing to educate their children through a distance education program. Given the significant shift concerning the geographical location of the respondents identified above, that is, from the traditional rural/remote to urban/regional settings, understanding the reason why distance education was selected as opposed to a conventional day school will equip educators to design more relevant learning, support and welfare programs.

Of the survey respondents, 81% identified having had their children previously enrolled in a conventional day school, and the remaining 19% had enrolled their child from their initial year of education, being prep level (students aged 5 years). Of the respondents who indicated having previously had their child enrolled in a conventional day school, 36% shifted their child's enrollment to distance education due to the child being bullied, Table 3. The survey did not allow a respondent to expand on the mode of bullying (online, physical or verbal). In addition, the present research study found that 14% of respondents stated that they moved their child from a conventional day school to distance education due to the child developing school anxiety and depression.

In considering that the principal reasons for parents selecting distance education was from bullying, anxiety, and depression, distance education providers may find that initial well-being support could significantly benefit newly enrolled students. There is, of course, the challenge to a distance educator to provide well-being support to a child who is working remotely; however, given the advances in technology, there are opportunities for distance educators to explore further opportunities to respond to student well-being. It is

The Urbanization of Distance Education in Australia

suggested that student well-being in distance education requires additional research.

The data presented in Table 3 shows that 28% of respondents selected distance education to improve their children's academic outcomes. Developing rigorous academic programs in a distance education program relies heavily on subject-teacher expertise. Teachers preparing academic learning material need to be equipped with an understanding of distance education pedagogies, with a thorough understanding of engaging children who work remotely. The role of the home tutor also plays a vital role in the academic outcomes achieved by a student enrolled in distance education, and it may benefit students where distance education providers provide training to the home tutors.

The research survey asked respondents who previously had a child enrolled in a conventional school if they were likely to re-enroll their child in a conventional school again. Analysis of the data, presented in Table 4, shows that 72.5% responded that they were either unlikely (37.5%) or would not (35%) enroll their child into a conventional school again, whereas 25% of respondents stated that they would consider a conventional school if the circumstances were right. Distance education is not the first choice for many families. However, once their student was enrolled, the parent found it a largely positive alternative to a conventional day school.

Analysis of the survey data found that there were secondary motivations for enrolling a child in distance education. As the research survey allowed for multiple responses, there were $n = 96$ responses. Of the responses, 28% selected distance education due to the flexible nature of the learning program, 21% to improve their child's academic outcomes, and 16.5% as they were unhappy with their child's previous school, see Table 5. Of the responses, 9.5% were motivated to enroll in distance education to improve their child's social connection.

Student Engagement

Irrespective of the learning context, student engagement is central to effective learning, student success, and student well-being (Maeher, 1984; Fredericks et al., 2004). Student engagement is defined by Axelson and Flick (2011, p. 38) as "how involved or interested students appear in their learning and how connected they are to their classes, their institutions, and each other." Various international

TABLE 3

Reasons for Moving From a Conventional Day School

Bullying Issues	Not Meeting My Child's Needs	My Child Suffers From Depression/ Anxiety	Too Many Distractions at School	Improved Academic Progress	The Travel Time Was Too Far	Due to My Child's Health Issues
36%	11%	14%	3%	28%	3%	3%

TABLE 4

The Likelihood That a Parent Would Re-Enroll Their Child Into a Conventional Day School

Likely	Unlikely	I Would Consider it if Circumstances Were Right	I Would Not Consider it at All
2.50%	37.50%	25%	35%

TABLE 5

Additional Motivations for a Parent Enrolling Their Child in Distance Education

	Flexible Learning	Improved Family Connection	To Spend More Time With My Children	Improved Academic Outcomes	Improve Social Connections	Unhappy With Previous School
$N = 96$ responses	28%	11.5%	13.5%	21%	9.5%	16.5%

TABLE 6

Parent Perception of Student Engagement

	Very High	High	Good	Low	Poor
Percent respondents	18.5%	7.5%	55.5%	11.0%	7.5%

studies have explored mechanisms for enhanced student motivations. However, a study by Murphy and Rodriguez-Manzanares (2009) analyzes teachers' perspectives on student motivation, including personal relationships, interactions and discussions, humor, teacher feedback, engaging learning, the pace of learning, and encouragement.

Of the survey respondents, 81.5% responded that they perceived their child's engagement in learning was a good or above level of engagement, with 18.5% responding that their child's engagement was low or poor, see Table 6. Maintaining student engagement in a distance education context is essential, and distance education providers may benefit by reflecting on the findings of Murphy and Rodriguez-Manzanares (2009).

Social Engagement

Within a conventional school context, classrooms and playgrounds facilitate the development of social competence. Kostelnik et al. (2014, p. 2) define social competence as "the knowledge and skills children need to achieve their goals and to interact with others effectively." Distance education lacks a visible interaction between the class teacher and between peers and has the potential to socially

isolate a child who is learning from home. While physically attending school creates opportunities for social engagement, analysis of the data from the present study suggests that students who study through distance education are not disadvantaged socially. In fact, as Participant 25 stated, "I had perceived DE as socially isolating before we started [but] my teen has more social interaction with different groups [whereas] when at school, it was just with the same group."

Distance education also offers opportunities for students to grow in social competence and confidence, as Participant 30 explained

[my child] was previously very shy and withdrawn. She has now grown in confidence and is able to communicate in a more confident and sophisticated level with adults. Her communication skills are excellent and she has lost the fear of her peers which enables greater creative and truthful expression.

This statement was supported by Participant 36, who stated:

It wasn't until we started schooling from home through [distance education] that we noticed a massive change in our daughter's temperament within the first 3 months. She was so much happier, less anxious, we watched her blossom as that pressure lifted from her shoulders.

Participant 13 shared that they had moved to distance education to develop academically as well as socially:

Yes! Day school broke one of our children. We enrolled them in [distance education] for Year 2, with that year spent mostly building their self-esteem, confidence, and motivation. Two years later, they've jumped 3-year levels, increased in self-confidence, and now enjoy learning.

The above parent statements show that distance education is not socially disadvantaging children. The research survey asked parents if they could identify a decline either socially or academically; of the responses, 95% of participants stated that there was no decline socially or academically. In addition, when parents were asked if they would recommend distance education to other parents, 88% responded that they would recommend distance education, and 12% stated that they might recommend distance education to other parents.

CURRENT CHALLENGES AND FUTURE OPPORTUNITIES

The recent pandemic resulted in schools across the globe rolling out "emergency remote education," whereby education institutes deployed a range of pedagogical approaches to enable ongoing teaching and learning to primary and secondary-aged students. While many of the "emergency remote learning" was rolled out haphazardly, with significant software companies developing and offering educational services (Williamson et al., 2020), analysis of these models and learning platforms will enhance the future of distance education. Zimmerman (2020, p. 1) states

Coronavirus ... has created a set of unprecedented natural experiments. For the first time, entire student bodies have been compelled to take all their classes online. So we

can examine how they perform in these courses compared to the face-to-face kind without worrying about the bias of self-selection. It might be hard to get good data if the online instruction only lasts a few weeks. However, at institutions that have moved to online-only for the rest of the semester, we should be able to measure how much students learn in that medium compared to the face-to-face instruction they received earlier.

Distance education opens a breadth of opportunities for primary and secondary school learners. One such example is within the learning area of language. There is a need for more language teachers in many countries, including Australia, Canada, the United Kingdom, and New Zealand (Swanson & Mason, 2018). Distance education opens an avenue for facilitating online language programs. A current example of this is a language provider of Mandarin whose teacher is based in Beijing and "zooms" into classrooms across the globe, providing students context to the study of the Mandarin language. Both distance education and conventional day schools have the opportunity to take a similar approach by engaging specialist teachers from across the globe in areas such as robotics, engineering, music, drama, and dance.

Distance education has the potential to enhance blended learning programs. Blended learning broadly refers to learning which includes more than one mode of learning and may be defined as "the thoughtful integration of classroom face-to-face instruction with online learning experiences" (Garrison & Kanuka, 2004). Blended learning combines asynchronous learning with the immediacy of classroom-based learning programs and opportunities for the growth and development of a learning community (Garrison & Kanuka, 2004). Internationally, there has been a shift among tertiary institutions toward the blended learning model (Jowsey et al., 2020). With an ever-changing educational landscape, it is recommended that Primary and Secondary learning providers seek to develop blended learning models.

CONCLUSION

This study's purpose was better to understand the reasons behind the urbanization of distance education. The data from this study reveals that 87% of respondents were located within an urban or large regional setting, with 49% residing within 100 km of Brisbane, the capital city of Queensland. As outlined in the introduction, distance education is defined as "an equity program for ... students who are geographically isolated or whose individual circumstances prevent them from regularly attending school" (https://education.nsw .gov.au/). The data within this research study contrasts this general definition and demonstrates a clear shift from the roots of correspondence education to rural and remote students. The present study defines "an educational program which is pedagogically designed so as to allow the student and educator to be spatially separatee." This changed definition clarifies that distance education is an equitable learning program for geographically isolated and urban students.

Analysis of survey data shows a significant proportion of parents selected distance education due to bullying issues at the child's previous school, along with parents seeking improved academic outcomes for their child. The data from this research found that, according to parents, 81.5% of children demonstrated good to very high levels of engagement. This level of engagement may indicate why 72.5% of parents were unlikely or would not consider enrolling their child in a conventional school again.

Distance education has the potential to continue to grow as more families realize that it is an equitable alternative to conventional school. With the rapid development of educational technology and high levels of academic and social engagement, distance education may become the first choice for parents when considering their child's education.

While the findings of this research study will assist distance education providers, researchers, and government organizations, it is essential to note that this was a small-scale research project, and further research is required to understand the shifting paradigm of distance education.

NOTE

1. For this paper, "parent" encompasses parent, carer, or guardian.

REFERENCES

Australian Bureau of Statistics. (2022). *Region summary: Queensland.* https://dbr.abs.gov.au/region.html?lyr=ste&rgn=3

Axelson, R., & Flick, A. (2010). Defining student engagement. *Change: The Magazine of Higher Learning, 43*(1), 38–43.

Bozkurt, A. (2019). From distance education to open and distance learning: A holistic evaluation of history, definitions, and theories. In S. Sisman-Ugur & G. Kurubacak (Eds.), *Handbook of research on learning in the age of transhumanism.* IGI Global.

Cunningham, K. S. (1931). *Primary education by correspondence.* Melbourne University Press.

Eppley, K., & Dudley-Marling, C. (2019). Does direct instruction work?: A critical assessment of direct instruction research and its theoretical perspective. *Journal of Curriculum and Pedagogy, 16*(1), 35–54.

Fereday, J., & Muir-Cochrane, E. (2006). Demonstrating rigor using thematic analysis: A hybrid approach of inductive and deductive coding and theme development. *International Journal of Qualitative Methods, 5*(1), 80–92.

Forlin, C., & Tierney, G. (2006). Accommodating students excluded from regular schools in schools of isolated and distance education. *Australian Journal of Education, 50*(1), 50–61.

Fredricks, J. A., Blumenfeld, P. C., & Paris, A. H. (2004). School engagement: Potential of the concept, state of the evidence. *Review of Educational Research, 74,* 59–109.

Garrison, D. R., & Kanuka, H. (2004). Blended learning: Uncovering its transformative potential in higher education. *Internet and Higher Education, 7,* 95–105.

Good Schools Guide. (2021). *Distance education.* https://www.goodschools.com.au/start-here/

choosing-a-school/special-needs/distance-education

Hannum, W. H., Irvin, M. J., Lei, P.-W., & Farmer, T. W. (2008). Effectiveness of using learner-centered principles on student retention in distance education courses in rural schools. *Distance Education, 29*(3), 211–229.

He, L., Yang, N., Xu, L., Ping, F., Li, W., Sun, Q., ... & Zhang, H. (2021). Synchronous distance education vs. traditional education for health science students: A systematic review and meta-analysis. *Medical Education, 55*(3), 293–308.

Independent Schools Queensland. (2021). Media release: More children are studying distance education in Queensland Independent schools during a pandemic. https://www.isq.qld.edu.au/publications-resources/posts/more-children-studying-via-distance-education-in-queensland-independent-schools-during-the-pandemic/

Jadambaa, A., Thomas, H., Scott J. G, Graves, N., Brain, D., & Pacella, R. (2020). The contribution of bullying victimization to the burden of anxiety and depressive disorders in Australia. *Epidemiology and Psychiatric Sciences, 29*(e54), 1–23.

Joffe, H. (2012). Thematic analysis. In D. Harper & A. R Thompson (Eds.), *Qualitative research methods in mental health and psychotherapy: A guide for students and practitioners* (pp. 210–223). John Wiley & Sons.

Jowsey, T., Foster, G., Cooper-Ioelu, P., & Jacobs, S. (2020). Blended learning via distance in pre-registration nursing education: A scoping review. *Nurse Education in Practice, 44*, 102775.

Kostelnik, M., Whiren, A., Soderman, A., Rupiper, M. L., & Gregory, K. (2014). *Guiding children's social development and learning.* Wadsworth.

Maehr, M. L. (1984). Meaning and motivation: Toward a theory of personal investment. *Research on Motivation in Education, 1*(4), 115–144.

Murphy, E., & Rodriguez-Manzanares, M. (2009). Teachers' perspective on motivation in high school distance education. *Journal of Distance Education, 23*(3), 1–24.

Naidu, S. (2017). How flexible is flexible learning, who is to decide, and what are its implications? *Distance Education, 38*(3), 269–272.

Persada, S. F., Prasetyo, Y. T., Suryananda, X. V., Apriyansyah, B., Ong, A. K., Nadlifatin, R., & Ardiansyahmiraja, B. (2022). How the education industries react to synchronous and asynchronous learning in COVID-19: Multigroup analysis insights for future online education. *Sustainability, 14*, 15288.

Rehn, N., Maor, D., & McConney, A. (2018). The specific skills required of teachers who deliver K–12 distance education courses by synchronous videoconference: Implications for training and professional development. *Technology, Pedagogy, and Education, 27*(4), 417–429.

Reiach, S., Averbeck, C., & Cassidy, V. (2012). The evolution of distance education in Australia. *The Quarterly Review of Distance Education, 12*(4), 247–252.

Shearer, R. L., Aldemir, T., Hitchcock, J., Resig, J., Driver, J., & Kohler, M. (2020). What students want: A vision of a future online learning experience grounded in distance education theory. *American Journal of Distance Education, 34*(1), 36–52.

Te Riele, K., Wilson, K., Wallace, V., McGinty, S. & Lewthwaite, B. (2017). Outcomes from flexible learning options for disenfranchised youth: what counts? *International Journal of Inclusive Education, 21*(2), 117–130.

Serdyukov, P. (2020). Asynchronous/synchronous learning chasm. In C. Sistek-Chandler (Ed.), *Exploring online learning through synchronous and asynchronous instructional methods.* IGI Global.

Stacey, E. (2005). The history of distance education in Australia. *The Quarterly Review of Distance Education, 6*(3), 253–259.

Stockard, J. (2011). Increasing reading skills in rural areas: An analysis of three school districts. *Journal of Research in Rural Education, 26*(8), 1–19.

Swanson, P., & Mason, S. (2018). *The world language teacher shortage: Taking a new direction.* American Council on the Teaching of Foreign Languages.

The Northern Territory Government (2021). Distance and online learning. https://nt.gov.au/learning/primary-and-secondary-students/distance-and-online-learning

Williamson, B., Eynon, R., & Potter, J. (2020). Pandemic politics, pedagogies, and practices: Digital technologies and distance education during the coronavirus emergency. *Learning, Media and Technology, 45*(2), 107–114.

Veletsianos, G., & Houlden, S. (2019). An analysis of flexible learning and flexibility over the last

40 years of distance education. *Distance Education, 40*(4), 454–468.

Zimmerman, J. (2020). Coronavirus and the great online-learning experiment: Let's determine what our students actually learn online. *The Chronicle of Higher Education.* https://ezproxy.csu.edu.au/login?url=https://www.proquest.com/trade-journals/coronavirus-great-online-learning-experiment/docview/2639988105/se-2

STRATEGIES FOR MANAGING THE CHALLENGES OF STUDENT VIRTUAL TEAMS IN HIGHER EDUCATION
A Case Study

Jill E. Nemiro, Anel Ayala, Jodee S. Lee, and Briseli San Luis
Cal Poly Pomona

> This paper describes a case study of one large asynchronous college-level organizational psychology class taught during COVID-19, in which a major intent was to develop virtual teamwork skills in students. A literature review yielded four challenges of virtual teams in higher education—communication, trust, connection and social bonding, and joint commitment and accountability. The course offered students an opportunity to authentically develop strategies to manage these challenges. Course design, team assignments, and instructional strategies utilized are described. Results from a survey completed by 89 (out of 115) students in the course revealed student-generated strategies and recommendations for virtual team collaboration.

Virtual teams have been defined as teams with members in which communication, tasks, and goals are accomplished primarily through technology and are contrasted with traditional teams that meet and accomplish work face to face (Nemiro, 2004). Over the last 20 years, the use of virtual teams has expanded in business settings, and so has the research investigating the effectiveness of virtual teams (Garro-Abarca et al., 2021). In higher educational settings, the coronavirus pandemic in 2020 generated an even more significant increase in the utilization of virtual or online learning as mandatory lockdowns were enforced globally, and faculty and students that were previously used to teaching and learning face to face were forced to transition to virtual instruction quickly and to adapt team assignments into virtual team assignments (Cornella-Dorda et al., 2020). However, more research on virtual teams in higher education is needed (Charteris et al., 2021; Jensen & Trespalacios, 2022).

To gain a more thorough understanding of how to effectively teach students to collaborate in virtual teams and to better prepare them for

---

• **Correspondence concerning this article should be addressed to:** Jill E. Nemiro, jenemiro@cpp.edu

The Quarterly Review of Distance Education, Volume 24(1), 2023, pp. 55–77
Copyright © 2023 Information Age Publishing, Inc.

ISSN 1528-3518
All rights of reproduction in any form reserved.

the changing workplace, the current paper describes a case study of one large asynchronous class in organizational psychology taught during the pandemic, where students were formed into virtual teams to complete a series of team assignments. After an initial review of the literature that yielded four significant challenges—communication, trust, connection and social bonding, and joint commitment and accountability—faced by students working in virtual teams in higher education, this case study paper then describes the instructional strategies that were used to help students deal with these challenges, and the strategies students shared they used and the recommendations they had for future students to meet these challenges as well.

PURPOSE OF THE CASE STUDY

Students developing virtual team skills and acquiring experience working in virtual teams have been increasingly important as many educational institutions, businesses, and organizations had to transition from face-to-face to completely remote work during the pandemic. While the popularity of remote work and virtual learning has risen throughout the years as technological advancements and developments have been made, teaching and learning during the pandemic were still challenging for educators and students. Despite its challenges, many businesses have realized the benefits of remote and hybrid work that occurred during the pandemic, and as a result, have continued to find ways to give employees the option of working remotely, moving into what has now been referred to as a new normal way of working (Brown, 2020; Dans, 2020; McKnight, 2021). Teaching students to work effectively in virtual teams is crucial to preparing students for their future careers. Research exploring the specific challenges of virtual teams and strategies used to meet those challenges in education is imperative to provide educators and students with the knowledge to make virtual team experiences within higher education effective while

also helping students learn valuable skills that will transfer into the workforce. Thus, the current paper attempts to answer the following questions:

1. What does the current literature reveal about the challenges faced by student virtual teams in higher education?
2. How can faculty design their courses to assist students in dealing with these challenges?
3. What strategies do students authentically develop and use to deal with these challenges?
4. What recommendations do students have for future students who will be required to work in virtual teams to meet these challenges?

LITERATURE REVIEW

Although online learning in higher education substantially increased during COVID-19, distance or online education, defined as "a method of teaching where the student and teacher are physically separated" (Kentnor, 2015, p. 22), has existed for some time. Distance education has been delivered over the years through correspondence education, educational radio and television programming, and, more recently, the creation of online programs offered through the internet. Today, online learning is "no longer a trend, but mainstream" (Kentnor, 2015, p. 22). As the world is becoming more dependent on the internet for essential tasks such as learning and working, students in higher education must learn how to adapt to the challenges of online learning and remote work. Some of the most commonly reported challenges experienced by students working in virtual teams are reviewed in the following sections.

Challenge of Communication

Despite technological advancements and communication tool developments, communication remains a challenge for students engaging in virtual teamwork in their courses. Recent research continues to validate that communication is a substantial issue for student virtual teams. Rauer et al. (2021) investigated cross-university virtual teamwork, where students from technical and economic fields and different universities and countries were asked to work on a global virtual team project together. The students from universities worldwide were assembled in mixed teams of four people to solve a parameterized, real-world case study and present their solutions to a remote evaluator. Students were also asked to rank their performance as well as their teammates. Mandatory student feedback was collected and anonymized, and the most important results from the feedback were summarized. Regarding previous international experience, only 40% indicated they had such experience, and only 8% gained the experience from their jobs. In contrast, 80% of the students said that this study's global virtual team project enhanced their international experience. Still, the most commonly reported challenge (mentioned by 21% of participants) was communication.

Challenges regarding communication between team members may arise even more so in an environment where students have no in-person or synchronous communication exchanges, for example, in a totally asynchronous course. In a study of the factors that inhibit and enhance creativity in asynchronous virtual teams, Ocker (2005) analyzed the communication transcripts over 6 months for 10 virtual teams composed of 47 MBA and MSIS graduate students who interacted solely via an asynchronous, computer conferencing system and were required to develop a new innovative product. Qualitative analysis of the transcripts revealed several challenges faced by the asynchronous teams that inhibited team creativity. These inhibiting factors included elements related to negative team dynamics, such as team member dominance (when one team member dominates, influences, and controls the design of the team's

work), domain knowledge (where there was an imbalance of knowledge of systems and related technologies among the members on the team); and downward norm-setting (where team members reduce their work performance to match the level of the least productive member on the team). In addition, teams low in creativity lacked a shared understanding of the project. As a result, these teams needed help reaching an agreement on a single cohesive design to move the work forward. Problems related to time pressure that impacted the team's ability to complete the work by the assigned due date and technical difficulties in terms of accessing the conferencing system were also inhibiting factors to creativity in these asynchronous teams. While these challenges were inhibitors specific to creativity, they also offer insight into problems asynchronous virtual teams face concerning communication and information exchange, both critical to team creativity (Nemiro, 2004; Nemiro, in press).

More recently, O'Connor et al. (2021) explored the challenges of large-class online education and experiential learning. Students completing a cross-cultural communication project were dispersed in two countries (the United States and Ireland). While communication issues in virtual teams are usually thought to occur between the team members, in this study, communication challenges between the instructor and students also surfaced, specifically the need for more precise and detailed instructions from instructors. The authors suggested that while this can also be a challenge in face-to-face student teams, it is even more so in asynchronous courses due to the lack of real-time engagement and the ability to ask questions during class.

Even when virtual teams have opportunities for synchronous online interactions, communication challenges still arise, for example, during synchronous virtual team meetings. Bailey-Hughes (2021) reported that faculty have witnessed that students on virtual teams often "lack accurate self-awareness of their communicative behaviors and their collective team dynamics during meetings" (p. 298). Bailey-Hughes (2021) discussed the challenge in communication in which information processing bias occurs and how information processing bias can result in poor decision-making. In these instances, team members discuss and share knowledge that everyone on the team already has rather than unique information that each specific team member may offer to the team. Having opportunities within virtual team meetings to have each member take the time to speak (referred to as go-arounds) may be a solution for information processing bias. It may equalize sharing and contributions within the team. However, Bailey-Hughes noted that in analyzing the recordings of student virtual team meetings, the students involved in those meetings rarely used that technique.

Communication challenges in virtual teams can also arise from teams comprised of members from differing cultural backgrounds. Having teams with diverse team members is encouraged as it leads to higher levels of creativity and critical thinking (Nemiro, in press); however, this same diversity can also create communication barriers. Especially for virtual teams that rely heavily on flat forms of communication (e.g., text, chat, email, or other written forms of communication exchange), the inability to have rich information exchanged in the message, for example, the absence of being able to read body language, may lead to conflict, confusion, and misunderstandings (Furamo & Pearson, 2006; Watson-Manheim & Belanger, 2002). In addition, some cultures may prefer direct, straightforward communication, while others favor more indirect forms of communication (Stoian, 2020). As a result of these differences in communication styles, conflict may arise between team members of differing cultural backgrounds. That conflict may be more challenging to resolve in virtual teams because of the lack of rich forms of communication (Flammia et al., 2016).

Challenge of Trust

Along with communication issues is the need for more trust in student virtual teams. Research in organizational settings has found that trust may be more challenging to establish and develop more slowly in virtual teams as opposed to in-person teams due to communication being less rich, more impersonal, and less predictable (Nemiro, 2000). Students in virtual teams find similar challenges concerning the development of team trust. For example, Grinnell et al. (2012) conducted a qualitative study on 30 students from eight online upper division Management and Marketing courses to analyze team behaviors and processes in virtual teams. One of the most common negative comments was on trust; for every positive comment relating to trust, there were seven negative comments.

A more recent study conducted by Mayfield and Valenti (2022) on virtual teams exploring team satisfaction, identity, and trust yielded the recurring theme of the challenge of trust. The study was assigned to 320 (304 after attrition) students pursuing an MBA degree taking a required teamwork and leadership course, in which eight courses were taught online and six face to face. The team evaluation survey, part of multiple self-assessments throughout the semester, was used for the study's research. Although team trust was lower midsemester in virtual teams compared to face-to-face teams, it did increase at the end of the semester, yet results were still lower than in face-to-face teams. Mayfield and Valenti (2022) suggested that trust is essential in virtual teams because work is completed online unobserved. The challenge of trust in virtual teams may be due to the lack of nonverbal signals (Flammia et al., 2016).

Challenge of Connection and Social Bonding

Another challenge that continues today, despite technological advances that allow for richer communication exchanges (Daft &

Strategies for Managing the Challenges of Student Virtual Teams in Higher Education

Engel, 1986), is that it may be easier for team members to feel detached or isolated from other team members while working virtually. The challenge of establishing interpersonal connections and social bonding is greater when students need to become more familiar with each other and without face-to-face meetings (Bailey-Hughes, 2021; O'Connor et al., 2021).

Kulturel-Konak et al. (2010) observed the issue of isolation and exclusion between teams with other subteams where they had been instructed to work together. In this study, teams were combined from two branch campuses of Pennsylvania State University in which different instructors taught students the same course. Four virtual teams of seven students were formed with students combined from both universities. Additional subteams were formed at each campus and asked to work with other subteams. Initially, all students were given an entrance survey to assess what they thought of virtual teams and if they had any prior experience with virtual teams. Results from the entrance survey indicated that while all students had face-to-face experience working in teams, none had prior virtual teamwork experience. Documents were then provided to help the teams establish team communication and operating norms and build trust. The virtual teams worked nine weeks to create a business report for a growing company's technology problems. An exit survey was then given to the teams. While the results indicated that more than 75% of students were enthusiastic and felt prepared for working in virtual teams in the future, a challenge was found in which subteams that felt connected and comfortable with one another excluded other subteams from communication about their work, which resulted in wasted effort and the duplication of assignments between subteams.

Results from Goold et al. (2006) illustrated how incorporating early activities to build connections between team members increased satisfaction with virtual teamwork, but that satisfaction faded as time passed. The authors held a 13-week online course in project management, in which students worked in virtual teams to complete a series of three project management topics. Topic 1, to be completed by week 4, asked students to get to know their virtual team members by having each team member complete a personality test, list their individual technical skills, and post an individual biography about themselves on a team discussion board. The second topic, due by week 8, required students to explore and post discussion board messages on the four core functions of project management—scope, time, cost, and quality (PMI Institute, 2000). The third topic, due by week 13 (the end of the semester), asked students to develop a project plan for a company. After each topic assignment, students were asked to complete anonymous surveys on their experiences working in virtual teams.

Survey results after Topic 1 (in week 4) indicated that students were generally positive about working on virtual teams and optimistic about the exercise requiring them to create and post individual biographies to the team's discussion board. Students felt the activity helped them get to know their team members and made the team more cohesive and trusting. However, subsequent survey results (after Topics 2 and 3, in weeks 8 and 13) showed that students' opinions of working in virtual teams declined, moving from being generally positive after Topic 1 to being marginally positive, with an increase in dissatisfaction after Topic 2, and only slightly more positive after Topic 3. Further, after Topic 3 (week 13), 15% of the students reported not liking working in their virtual team. Goold et al. (2006) concluded that while students may benefit from participating in activities to build connections, these exercises should be required throughout the semester, not just at the beginning. While personal connection and a social bond can be built in virtual teams, it may take longer and require a more concerted effort.

Logemann et al. (2022) studied how virtual collaboration and communication in a project (Project X) was used to build emotional connection and compassion among team members and offer emotional support during the COVID-19 health crisis, which required people to suddenly socially distance and isolate at home. Project X is a collaborative online international learning (COIL) program that helps students develop virtual intelligence, digital communication, and intercultural competency skills. COIL projects, such as Project X, involve students from across the globe working on assignments virtually through collaborative technologies. In 2020, Project X involved 530 students from 16 institutions in seven countries (Finland, France, Germany, India, Lithuania, Spain, and the United States). Students were assigned to virtual teams of five to six members, with each team member coming from a different location and university. The virtual teams collaborated for 6 weeks through team collaboration platforms and video conferencing tools (e.g., Slack and Zoom) to research and write a report on a business case. Three weeks into the 6-week project, the COVID-19 pandemic hit. At that time, all the participating universities shut their campuses and sent students and faculty home to work and learn remotely. Project X faculty members were then uniquely positioned to develop a study on how global virtual collaboration in a crisis could be used to build connections in virtual teams. To explore this, a postproject survey was given to all students, and 440 (out of the 530) students completed the survey. Questions on the survey asked students about the degree of emotional investment or connection and team-belonging they had in their teams. Based on the survey responses, teams were classified as either low-belonging, medium-belonging, or high-belonging. The survey data revealed that the members of high-belonging teams felt more at ease speaking up and asking for help, felt more valued, and felt like they had more support for their ideas (referred to as inclusion). High-belonging teams also reported that they enjoyed their virtual experiences and found them interesting and fun (copresence). Open-ended comments from the teams suggested more overall positivity in high-belonging teams compared to the medium

or low-belonging teams. Logemann et al.'s (2022) findings revealed that virtual teams could build an emotional and personal connection by ensuring inclusion and copresence through technology but achieving that personal bond may remain a challenge for some teams (e.g., low- and medium-belonging teams) even during a crisis.

Mayfield and Valenti (2022) explored team identity in virtual teams. Team identity has been referred to as a team member's sense of connectedness to the other members of their team and the value they derive from being a team member (Ashforth & Mael, 1989; Ellemers et al., 2013). Mayfield and Valenti hypothesized that initial levels of team identity would be higher for face-to-face student teams than for virtual student teams but that the difference would dissipate over time. The study involved 320 MBA students in 63 teams, with 120 taking the course face to face and 200 engaging in online coursework. The teams worked together for a 15-week semester, and students were given a survey assessing their attitudes toward their team at the middle and end of the semester. The study also explored team satisfaction and trust (previously discussed).

Interestingly, the researchers found that while ratings of team trust and team satisfaction were higher initially in face-to-face teams versus online teams, those differences diminished over time. However, ratings of team identity continued to be higher in face-to-face teams than in online teams, and that difference was held through the end of the semester. The authors suggested that using less rich communication channels (methods that lack nonverbal cues and can hide feelings or emotions) may necessitate that more time than 15 weeks in a semester for virtual teams to form team identity.

Challenge of Joint Commitment and Accountability

Accountability within student teams has long been a complaint of students in teams, whether in-person or virtual. However, accountability is an even more significant challenge for virtual teams, where there can be a tendency to drop out of the interaction virtually. Team members may need regular in-person or synchronous meetings to reach or connect with team members.

In a study that investigated the experience of students learning in virtual teams (Goold et al., 2006), students were enrolled in an online Project Management and Information Systems course. Twenty-one virtual teams of seven students each were asked to complete online learning activities and solve project management tasks for a telecommunications company. The project included three topic modules, and students completed a survey following each module asking about their experiences working within a virtual team and their preferred technology tools. Survey results showed that while students enjoyed the experience of working in virtual teams, face to face was still favored. Because virtual teams and online learning generally require self-motivation, some students became frustrated when they felt some of their team members did not participate or procrastinated. Results from the first survey, in which students were asked to write what the best and worst things were about online group work, yielded several issues relating to motivation and accountability, such as discussion response time delay, lack of team members' timely participation, and team members waiting until the last minute to submit their work. The second survey results also mentioned team members not participating or joining discussions right before deadlines. In addition, student comments indicated dissatisfaction with unreachable team members, leaving other team members to do all the work.

Other challenges relevant to joint commitment and accountability emerged in a study by Cleary and Slattery (2009). Over three semesters, technical communication students from the University of Limerick in Ireland and the University of Florida in the United States joined student teams to complete three projects. The projects asked student teams to first design websites and brochures on intercultural communication and then write a report about the collaborative technologies they used. Across the three projects, teams experienced challenges with joint commitment and accountability due to uncooperative and non-participating team members, differences in life and work experience between younger and older team members, and the differences in time zones between where the team members resided.

Research has begun to explore strategies that can be used to help students overcome these challenges (Davis & Zigurs, 2008; Flammia et al., 2016; He et al., 2008; Kohut, 2012; Kulturel-Konak et al., 2010; Logemann et al., 2022; O'Connor et al., 2021; Sanders et al., 2015). This case study extends that research. The following sections will first describe the course and then outline a series of instructional and student-generated strategies and recommendations from the course. These strategies may be useful across other disciplines and in other courses as well.

DESCRIPTION OF THE COURSE

Course Content and Delivery Mode and Formation of Virtual Teams

Virtual teamwork was part of a course on organizational psychology taught at Cal Poly Pomona (CPP) in the Spring of 2022 during a 16-week semester. The course content included topics on (a) individuals in organizations (e.g., workplace happiness, culture, and diversity, decision-making processes, emotions at work, motivation and job design, personality, skills and abilities, and values); (b) work groups and teams, team effectiveness and team building; and (c) organizational strategy and structure.

The course was designed and delivered as a fully asynchronous or online, meaning all class requirements were completed online. Students did not need to come to campus for any portion of this course and were not required to be online during a specified class time. However, students were assigned to virtual teams and required to regularly meet synchronously in a virtual format at a time of their choosing to complete the virtual team assignments in the course.

The course material was delivered through CPP's Canvas Learning Management System. Modules on Canvas included prerecorded lectures, assigned readings, relevant Ted Talks and other videos, individual activity assignments, quizzes, and a series of assignments to be completed by students in virtual teams. To ensure clarity, students were provided with written guidelines, a video explanation recorded by the course instructor, and a sample paper for each virtual team assignment in the course.

The instructor formed virtual teams of three to five members, matched based on students' self-reported availability to virtually meet synchronously. Through CPP's Zoom technology, virtual teams were encouraged to meet weekly (at their common self-reported available time). Topics and agenda items for suggested discussion at these meetings were listed in the course syllabus.

Virtual Team Assignments

Although students were required in the course to do other individual-based assignments (e.g., individual application activities, discussion board posts, and quizzes), the virtual teams in the course were required to complete a virtual team project, which included the following elements: a team charter, team proposal, three virtual team activities, and a team final paper. In these assignments, each team could apply course content to real-world problems in organizations of their choice. Each team selected a topic within the field of organizational psychology to explore and then created an interview protocol to gather information about that topic from real-world managers. Each team member then independently explored that topic and used the team interview protocol to interview a manager of their choice. Then, the entire team came together to discuss the findings (confidentially) and make recommendations for further action based on the theories discussed in the course. The assignments had two main goals—to explore a specific area within the field of organizational psychology in more depth and through the eyes of real-world managers and to help students develop and practice virtual teamwork skills necessary for their professional lives. Each of the virtual team assignments is described in further detail.

In the *team charter* assignment, each team outlined their agreed-upon communication and project and task management norms they would follow for working together. For communication norms, the team was to list each communication method they would use to communicate with one another and then outline the norms around when members would be expected to be available to participate in or check communication from each method and describe any other protocols the team established for the use of each communication tool. Teams were encouraged to have asynchronous (such as group chat or text, email, or Google Docs) and synchronous methods (e.g., Zoom or FaceTime team meetings) in their communication plan. The charter was the first virtual team assignment in the course, due at the end of week four.

Also, in the team charter assignment, teams drafted project and task management norms around the following areas: (a) proposed deadlines for subsequent elements in the virtual team project and under what circumstances the team might adjust these deadlines; (b) accountability norms, including both positive actions to keep all members on task and responsible (e.g., suggested meetings, check-ins, reminders), and consequences for team members who miss deadlines, do not complete their assigned tasks, or do not contribute equitably; (c) tool(s) through which the team would create, edit, and revise the team proposal and final paper assignments (all team members needed to have access to the tools); (d) the method used to ensure all team members had approved the final revision of an assignment before it was uploaded to Canvas, and the plan for turning in assignments (e.g., Who will turn it in? Who will verify it has been turned in?)

In the *team proposal* assignment, each team included a brief description of the topic they chose to explore, followed by the proposed interview protocol the team developed for the interviews with their managers. All team members used the same interview questions for each interview, and protocols had to be approved by the course instructor before interviews began. Revisions were requested to assist the team in creating open-ended questions that focused on the topic(s) the team has proposed to explore.

Three *virtual team activities* were required. The interview progress check-in activity asked teams to report on the progress of each team member concerning the completion or expected completion date of the interview and transcription of interview data and to include any assistance they may need from the instructor. The team building activity was created for the virtual teams to experience a team building activity together, during the week the class was exploring team effectiveness and team building (week 12). The team final paper progress check-in activity asked teams to report on the team's progress on the team final paper; the tasks the team still had to do to complete the assignment, how and by when the team would accomplish those tasks; and what assistance the team might need from the instructor to complete the team final paper.

The team final paper included three major sections: (a) a description of the job title and general work responsibilities of the managers interviewed; (b) a description of issues or problems the managers faced concerning the topic under study in the paper; and any actions taken by the managers to deal with these issues (verified with evidence from the interview data); and (c) the team's recommendations (applying the course content) to assist the managers in further solving their issues or problems.

Instructional Strategies Used to Build Effective Virtual Teams

In the design and implementation of the course, instructional strategies were used to help students manage the challenges they may face in working on virtual teams. The strategies used are described in relation to each of the challenges that emerged during the literature review—communication, trust, connection and social bonding, and joint commitment and accountability.

Instructional Strategies for the Challenge of Communication

Communication is a key issue for virtual teams, as, without it, misunderstandings, confusion, and conflict can result. Several virtual communication strategies were used in the class to stay in contact and monitor the teams' progress. First, Sunday videos, brief weekly videos where the instructor reviewed what the students would need to accomplish during the week and offered general feedback and tips to teams, were recorded and posted on Canvas. In addition, a student assistant sent out Wednesday email reminders on what was due on Friday, along with a special note of encouragement. Periodic classwide Canvas announcements were also used to provide additional feedback and information to the virtual teams.

Further, at the beginning of the semester, the instructor sent out a Canvas announcement listing the teams, their members, and their common virtual meeting time. It encouraged the teams to get acquainted, exchange contact information, and read one another's discussion board introduction posts. The instructor was available on Zoom for 4 hours each week to assist students with their concerns or questions, and a student assistant was also available 1 hour per week. To meet students' varying schedules, these virtual office hours were split over 3 days and included morning, afternoon, and evening times.

Another critical element for an effective virtual team, or any team for that matter, is to create agreed-upon team norms for communication. As previously mentioned, the virtual team charter assignment led students through the process of developing team communication norms. In the team charter, students were asked to list all the communication tools their team found most suitable and would use and to outline when members would be accessible on these tools, how often they would check in, and the protocols or netiquette rules that would guide their communication behaviors for each tool.

Students were encouraged to use various communication tools, including asynchronous (email, Google Docs) and synchronous (Zoom) tools. To maintain frequent synchronous communication, teams were encouraged to meet regularly through Zoom (about 10 times during the semester at their own scheduled times). The topic of discussion and suggested agenda items for these team meetings were listed for students in the course syllabus. When team members had difficulty getting in touch with one another initially or maintaining consistent communication, the instructor intervened to assist students in getting in touch with each other.

Since technology is how virtual teams get their work done, to be an effective virtual team, each team member has to have access to needed technology and should be provided with appropriate IT training and support. Fortunately, as students of CPP, many technology tools were available, as were the resources for technological support and training, which were easily located on the course Canvas site. Further, the instructor and two student assistants provided further technological support as best they could.

Instructional Strategies for the Challenge of Trust

Trust between members on student virtual teams can take longer to build because of the need for in-person communication. In addition, because the teams in this class were temporary and would only exist within the context of a single course and then disband after the course was over, it was important to assist the teams with building swift trust (Meyerson et al., 1996).

In forming the teams, the instructor asked the class if any students had previously worked with other individuals in the class and would like to be placed on teams to work with them. All these requests were honored, as one way to build swift trust is to work with one who has had positive experiences in the past. However, most teams were formed based on the students' self-reported availability (time and day) for meeting virtually. For the most part, this strategy was useful in building trust, as team members knew that the individuals they were working with would be available at the same time they were.

One of the problems with virtual teams has been that communication through information technology eliminates some of the information or media richness (Daft & Lengel, 1986) that can be shared between team members when they work together in person. Contextual factors such as nonverbal communication (e.g., tone of voice, gestures, or facial expressions) are stripped away, leading to potential misunderstandings or distrust among virtual team members. As mentioned, students were encouraged to use various communication tools, including asynchronous and synchronous. Rich synchronous communication tools like Zoom offer students the ability to build trust by being able to hear and see one another while having private conversations, engaging in small group work in breakout rooms, or creating joint designs on a collaborative whiteboard (Reiter-Palmon et al., 2021).

To encourage synchronous interactions within the virtual teams, the instructor created a video outlining two potential procedures the teams could choose from in working on the final virtual team paper assignment. One was called the "joint work" procedure, in which teams worked synchronously on all sections of the final paper. The second approach was called the "modular approach" (Nemiro, 2004) and outlined a process involving alternating periods of working independently and working together as a team to complete the final paper. Although the amount of time spent working synchronously together varied between the two approaches, time spent together in synchronous Zoom work sessions was emphasized in each. During these meetings, students were to brainstorm and discuss their ideas, and through these interactions, trust was built. As will be seen in the results section, the two most frequent communication methods used by the student teams were Google Docs and Zoom team meetings. These Zoom team meetings helped students build trust because they could hear and see one another while sharing their opinions and ideas.

Even though the virtual team assignment was a team assignment, each team member had to interview a manager of their choice independently. Teams were then required to complete a progress report on the completion of the interviews, and as team members completed their interviews, they demonstrated they could be trusted with their work. In addition, the team progress report on the final team paper was another opportunity to build team trust. One element that trust is based on is accountability (Nemiro, 2004), and outlining in the final team paper progress report what had been done, what still needed to be completed, and who and how that would be done set the stage for accountability and trust.

Instructional Strategies for the Challenge of Connection and Social Bonding

When virtual teams are initially being formed, it is important to take the time to build interpersonal bonds and task connections between team members. Moreover, once teams are up and running, it is still important to continue to have ways to develop further and maintain team connections. In this class, we developed an initial connection and understanding by holding a synchronous orientation at the beginning of the course, where the instructor introduced the course and answered students' questions. Additionally, all students were asked to introduce themselves virtually in an introductory discussion post. Members of the same virtual team were required to read the

team members' introductions and were encouraged to hold an introductory team meeting through Zoom. To maintain connection throughout the semester, teams were encouraged to continue to meet through Zoom during the semester at their own scheduled time. Further, the virtual team-building activity was a fun bonding experience for the teams.

Instructional Strategies for the Challenge of Joint Commitment and Accountability

Another critical element for an effective virtual team, or any team for that matter, is to create a joint level of dedication and commitment among all the members of the team and to establish accountability to ensure team members contribute equitably to the team's work as well (Nemiro, 2004). As previously mentioned, the virtual team charter assignment led students through the process of developing team norms. Each team was required to establish its own set of accountability norms (positive norms to ensure accountability and consequences for nonperforming team members) as a key part of their team's project and task management norms. The instructor abided by each team's unique set of accountability norms.

An instructional strategy that helped keep the student teams accountable and on track was the requirement that teams could only begin their interviews with their managers once the instructor had reviewed, revised, and approved each team's protocol. Getting all the teams approved took about a month, and they appreciated getting feedback and revisions on their protocols. The progress check-in virtual team activity assignments (interview and final team paper) also helped to keep team members accountable. They kept the instructor informed of each team's progress and what the teams needed. Finally, even though there were two assistant student graders in the course, the instructor graded all virtual team assignments; student graders handled reviewing only individual activity and discussion post assign-

TABLE 1

Summary of Instructional Strategies Used

Challenge	Instructional Strategies Used
Communication	• Sunday weekly overview videos by the instructor. • Wednesday reminder emails by a student assistant. • Initial Canvas team announcement. • Use of Canvas announcements throughout the semester. • Four hours of instructor and 1 hour of student assistant weekly office hours spread across different days and times. • The virtual team charter assignment required asking teams to outline their communication norms. • Encouraged teams to use asynchronous and synchronous communication tools. • Encouraged frequent Zoom team meetings (provided topics and suggested agenda for meetings in the course syllabus). • Encouraged use of CPP-provided technology. • Provided information on CPP IT support and training on Canvas. • Instructors and student assistants provided additional IT support.
Trust	• Formed teams based on student requests or self-reported availability. • The instructor provided a video outlining suggested workflow procedures for virtual teams (joint work or modular), which emphasized time for synchronous brainstorming and discussion. • Each team member had an individual task to complete (their interview). • Two virtual team progress report activities (interview and final team paper) set the stage for trust based on accountability.
Connection and social bonding	• Initial synchronous orientation session held by instructor and student assistants. • Students were required to introduce themselves in a discussion board post, and members of the same team were required to read team members' introductory posts. • Teams were encouraged to hold an initial get-to-know-one-another Zoom meeting before beginning their assignments. • Encouraged frequent Zoom team meetings (provided topics and suggested meeting agenda). • Virtual team building activity assignment offered students a fun bonding experience.
Joint accountability and commitment	• Virtual team charter assignment required asking teams to outline their project and task management norms, especially accountability. • Instructor approval of the interview protocol and consent form was required before team members could begin their interviews. • Two virtual team progress report activities (interview and final team paper) set the stage for accountability. • The instructor graded all virtual team assignments.

ments. By having the instructor grade all virtual team assignments, the instructor could take a proactive approach and request meetings with teams that needed or had asked for assistance.

Summary of Instructional Strategies Used

Table 1 summarizes the instructional strategies used to help students deal with the challenges of communication, trust, connection, social bonding, and joint commitment and accountability.

METHODS

Participants

Participants were recruited from an organizational psychology asynchronous course

Strategies for Managing the Challenges of Student Virtual Teams in Higher Education

taught in the Spring 2022 semester in the Psychology Department at Cal Poly Pomona. The course was a large section, with 115 students enrolled. All students were at either junior (26 out of 115) or senior (89 out of 115) level standing. To complete the virtual team assignments, the 115 students were divided into 28 virtual teams (each with between three to five members). Near the end of the semester, an announcement was posted on the course Canvas site inviting all 115 students (if they were 18 or above) to participate in a survey on their experiences with virtual teams in the course. Out of the 115 students invited, 89 students completed the survey (a 77% response rate). Students who completed the survey received five extra credit points in the course. If a student did not want to participate in the survey, an alternative extra credit assignment was also offered, worth the same amount of extra credit points.

The survey link was opened to students on the course Canvas site at the end of week 11 and remained accessible to students until the 16-week course was over. The survey was created on Qualtrics, Provo, UT. Students were presented with an informed consent form after clicking on the link. Students who decided to complete the survey then clicked on the arrow button to consent to participation and were presented with the survey.

Survey Measure

The survey included open-ended questions asking participants about the strategies their virtual team used to work effectively together virtually, the types of communication tools or technology apps they found most helpful while working virtually with the members of their virtual team, and what recommendations they would have for future students in the course who have to work on virtual teams. One close-ended question asked students to select all of the communication tools their team used to communicate and collaborate on the virtual team assignments in the course. Tools listed included: Google Docs, Zoom, GroupMe, Dis-

cord, Microsoft Teams, Text, FaceTime, and other write-ins. No demographic or identifying information was solicited on the survey to ensure anonymity.

Data Analysis Techniques

A thematic analysis was conducted on the open-ended, qualitative student responses to the questions on strategies used and suggested recommendations for future students. Counting was then used to indicate the number of quotes related to each code. All three researchers (faculty member and two student research assistants) were involved in the thematic analysis process and reviewed the quotes for each theme to select quotes they felt were the most illustrative examples. Quotes in the paper's results section were selected by at least two (and often all three) of the researchers.

To analyze the open-ended responses to the question which asked students to write in the types of communication tools and technology apps they found most useful, a list was created with the names of all tools and apps mentioned. Then, the frequency or number of times each tool or app was mentioned was calculated. For the close-ended question, which asked students to check which tools they used—Google Docs, Zoom, GroupMe, Discord, Microsoft Teams, Text, FaceTime, and Other—the frequency or number of times each tool was selected was calculated. In addition, student team charter assignments were reviewed, a list of all the tools and apps teams suggested they would use to work together was created, and the number of teams that mentioned each communication tool was calculated.

RESULTS

In the results section that follows, first, the communication tools used by the teams will be discussed. Then, the findings that emerged from what the students shared about strategies they used to work effectively together, and recommendations they had for future students working in virtual teams, will be organized around the challenges revealed in the literature section—communication, trust, connection, and social bonding, and joint commitment and accountability.

Communication Tools Used

Students were required to complete a team charter assignment, due by the end of the fourth week in the 16-week semester. In the charter, one section asked each team to list each communication method it planned to use to communicate with one another. A review of the 28 team charters in the class (one charter per team) showed what communication tools the teams planned to use in working virtually together on their team assignments. All teams indicated they planned to use Zoom and Google Docs. Other popular tools were GroupMe and Cal Poly Pomona's (CPP) internal email system (mentioned by 21 teams) and Text (planned to be used by 17 teams). Less frequently mentioned communication tools included the Inbox in CPP's Canvas learning management system for the course (4 teams); Discord (3 teams); and one team for each of the following communication tools—FaceTime, Phone Call, Google Calendar, Google Slides, Microsoft Teams, and Cozi Family Organizer.

While the team charters included information on the communication tools students planned to use (as it was each team's first assignment and was turned in at the end of week four), the survey results (from data that was collected from the end of week 11 until the completion of the 16-week course) reported what communication tools the students did use, and which they found were most helpful. Results are shown in Table 2.

For the most part, students used Google Docs, Zoom, GroupMe, and Text to communicate and accomplish their virtual team assignments. The students viewed GroupMe as the most helpful tool, followed by Google Docs, Zoom, and Text. While Discord was used sparingly, for those that did, the majority thought it was helpful. Discord can be helpful, especially with the organization, because one can create different channels. However, students may have found it overwhelming or intimidating to navigate initially. FaceTime was not considered helpful by the majority of students who used it. Microsoft Teams, a tool for collaborative work that Cal Poly Pomona offers students access to, was not used at all. This may indicate the need for better preparation and training in university-sponsored communication

TABLE 2

Communication Tools Used and Found Most Useful

Communication Tool	Number of Students Used Tool (n = 89)*	# of Students Who Found Tool Most Helpful (n=88)**
Google Docs	86	36
Zoom	65	28
GroupMe	59	42
Text	39	23
Discord	9	6
FaceTime	7	2
Microsoft Teams	0	0
Other	0	0

Note: *89 students answered this question. **88 students answered this question.

tools as part of the curriculum for online courses. Tools that Cal Poly Pomona does offer students access to that were used by students included Google Docs and Zoom. It was encouraging that many students reported using Zoom (65), as it was a tool that allowed for richer forms of synchronous communication than did some of the other communication tools. Students did not write in any other forms of communication tools.

Student-Generated Strategies Used and Suggested Recommendations

Described in this section are the themes that emerged from the analysis of the qualitative responses to the question asking students to share strategies their team used to help the team work effectively together and to the question asking students for recommendations they had for future students in this course who have to work on virtual teams. The findings are discussed around the previously identified challenges—communication, trust, connection and social bonding, and joint commitment and accountability. As expected, many of the recommendations are similar to students' strategies to manage these challenges while working in virtual teams during the course.

Communication

Strategies. Nearly all students who participated in the survey (86 out of the 88 students who answered this question, or 98%) mentioned strategies to assist with communication. One strategy mentioned by over half of the student respondents (46 students) was the frequent use of group messaging tools (i.e., GroupMe, Discord, or text) to stay in contact and to send out regular updates and reminders about deadlines; and establish norms around when to check these tools as well. For example, one student shared, "Some strategies we have been implementing is to start a group chat to discuss what we will be doing for the week and provide each other with updates on the group assignments/projects." Another student

further specified how often the team was to check the group chat, "We decided to use GroupMe and text message chat where we would all be in contact about any questions we had. We also would check our chats at least once a day to see if anything was new."

Another strategy was regularly holding scheduled synchronous Zoom team meetings, as mentioned by 25 students. Teams in the class were matched based on their self-reported availability to meet out of class. So students could set up schedules for meetings in advance, as this one student shared, "In the first meeting, we scheduled every Zoom meeting we would have and what would be done in that meeting. This way, we were all free and prepared to work on the assignment." Sticking to the same time and day for each meeting was key, as illustrated by this student, "We kept the Zoom meeting times the same on the same day and scheduled them all out at once."

A final communication strategy mentioned by 15 students was for their team to maintain an overall emphasis on constant, frequent, and open communication, as these students shared: "We communicated often on what we needed to do and what we were going to do"; and "I think just being open and communicative about any issues we are having." One student expressed this strategy as the need to overcommunicate, "I have to say over communication, we didn't allow for any guessing and assumptions to be made."

Recommendations. Echoing the strategies students shared that they used in working virtually, the first recommendation for future students (mentioned by 25 students) to ensure effective and smooth virtual teamwork was that team members need to view communication as essential and key, and actively keep communicating, making communication frequent, regular, consistent, and open. For example, one student shared, "Everyone will have different experiences when working with virtual teams. You may find it really helpful or you may not like working in it because you get to do all the work, but communication within your team really helps." Another student shared, "Communicate often and let others know where you are in terms of your work progress and your groupwork will go much more smoothly."

Nine students suggested that future students not be afraid to be vocal and direct in team communications, especially concerning unresponsive or underperforming team members. One student shared, "Don't be afraid to be direct with people who aren't answering. We live in a time where everyone has their phone in their hand 24/7." Another student shared, "Be more vocal when you feel that the work distribution isn't equally distributed. I regret not being open with my team and discussing more of work effort." Students suggested sending reminders as effective way to voice concerns, "Don't be afraid to let other group members know if you need help or to offer others help through friendly reminders." Reminders can also ensure all team members agree with the team's work and deadlines, as indicated in this student's comment, "Don't be afraid to send out reminder messages! It is easy to think everyone is on the same page when things are due but always expect others to be confused!"

Trust

Strategies. Only eight (out of the 88 students who answered this question, or 9%) offered specific strategies to build team trust. The team charter assignment was recognized as a useful tool to assist with trust based on accountability, as two students shared: "We stuck by the group charter"; and "The team charter helped us build trust and stay on track as well as track our progress." In addition, six students mentioned having norms for respectful, constructive, and inclusive decision-making as a way to build trust within the team. For example, one student shared, "We used constructive criticism and genuine thought and consideration for each other's efforts." Another student commented, "We would discuss each assignment with each other to see if we agreed on the answer."

Recommendations. In dealing with the members of one's team, seven students recommended being respectful and patient with one another and their schedules; and being open-minded and flexible with others' work styles, as shared by this student, "Be upfront about the way you like to work, but also be flexible if other members don't work that way." In addition, being open to working on a virtual team was recommended to assist with team dynamics and trust, as this student shared, "Being open to it, it is something that many find nerve-wracking and uncomfortable so know that you are not alone in feeling that way and just be open to giving it your best shot." Keeping the size of the team small was also recommended by one student.

Connection and Social Bonding

Strategies. Only a few students offered specific strategies for building connection and social bonding in their teams, primarily doing so by providing help and support when their team members needed it. This was illustrated by the following student comments, "I like how we all help each other out and have a support network"; "It provided a group that I could turn to for help"; and "I felt supported by my team members aside from the classwork, if any of us had a question, we knew we could ask each other."

Recommendations. Four students suggested it would benefit teams to take time to develop connections between team members by having fun and enjoying the team's interactions and work, and not being shy. For example, students shared: "Enjoy and have fun, get to know your peers, and always work as a team"; and "Don't be shy, at first it might seem horrible if you're a shy person, but it gets easier, and once you warm up to others it's actually not bad at all." To further build connection, a student suggested discussing individual team members' work habits, strengths, and weaknesses in synchronous meetings to understand one another better, as illustrated in this comment: "I would recom-

Strategies for Managing the Challenges of Student Virtual Teams in Higher Education

mend getting to know each other. This may seem odd, but having a Zoom meeting where everyone discusses their schoolwork habits (such as people who prefer working on assignments ASAP versus last minute), strengths and weaknesses, etcetera."

Joint Commitment and Accountability

Strategies. Forty-one percent of the student respondents (36 out of 88 students that responded to this question) mentioned specific strategies to assist their teams in managing joint commitment and accountability while working on the team's project and related tasks. The use of a document-sharing application, primarily Google Docs, was mentioned by 12 students as a specific useful strategy for managing the team's work. For example, one student shared, "We made a document so everyone could access the work, and it helped individuals who needed more time to work on it and those who wanted to finish their part beforehand."

Creating team deadlines for assignments before formal course deadlines to encourage early completion of the work was a strategy mentioned by nine students. Two examples of student comments were: "We all came up with specific deadlines together to get our parts of the work done"; and "Getting ahead of scheduled time frames as most of us have work that can get in the way of group work sometimes."

Eight students mentioned the strategy of assigning specific roles and delegating tasks to individual team members as a helpful way to manage the challenge of accomplishing the team's work, as illustrated by these students' comments: "I think that it was very helpful to assign tasks to each person as it gave a clearer goal to each person. It helped ease the confusion of what was due and when it should be accomplished"; and "After each meeting we posted what was covered and what we would do as far as individual tasks."

For each virtual team assignment in the course, students were provided with written guidelines, a video explanation recorded by the course instructor, and a sample paper. Three students recognized these clear assignment guidelines and instructions as a useful strategy in managing their team's work, as illustrated by these student comments: "We also had specific requirements of each assignment"; and "Clear instructions was the best method for effectively working together."

Four students mentioned the specific strategy of splitting the work evenly among team members, as illustrated by these students' comments: "We would split the work evenly so it was fair to everyone"; and "We have tried to hold people accountable by making sure we all split up work evenly."

Recommendations. Fifty student respondents offered recommendations for future students in the course to assist with establishing a joint level of commitment and accountability in their virtual teams. The first recommendation, shared by four students, was to have a general plan for the team's work and keep the work organized and stay up to date on completion of the work, as illustrated in these student comments: "Stay organized"; "Make sure they plan out with their groups what they are going to do"; and "Make sure you stay up to date with your team. It is easy to forget you have assignments due and just forget about having to do work in general."

Twelve students recognized the importance of setting and staying on top of deadlines and even striving to finish the work early, ahead of those deadlines. For example, one student shared, "Set deadlines and stay on top of them." Yet another student suggested, "Schedule being done with an assignment a few days before the actual due date as it then gives you some wiggle room to finish the assignment." In addition to setting deadlines, nine students recommended creating workable schedules (agreed-upon days and times) for team meetings from the very beginning of the team's inception, as suggested by this student, "Come up with a set time to meet right away. 1st thing you should do." Finding team members with similar schedules to collaborate with was another related recommendation, as indicated by these students' comments, "Find people with a similar schedule to you"; and "Make sure you guys have similar schedules."

To further assist with establishing accountability and an equitable workload across all team members, seven students shared that placing an overall emphasis on holding team members accountable and having reliable teammates was key to the success of a virtual team. This general emphasis on accountability was illustrated in these concise student recommendations, "Just to hold each other accountable"; "Always take accountability; it's a group effort"; and "Have reliable teammates."

Additional specific recommendations to achieve accountability included (a) doing one's part of the team's work (mentioned by seven students), as illustrated by this comment, "The only tip I would have is to pull your own weight and to do the work that you are designated to do. This way everything is even, and everyone has earned their own points instead of more of the work falling on other team members"; (b) assigning team members clear roles, duties, and work tasks (suggested by five students), as described in this response, "One tip that came from the professor is assigning each member a duty. I think that has really helped my team and I to stay on track and remind each other of what is due or soon due"; and (c) seeking out assistance from the professor or student assistant when needed, as shared by two students and expressed in this quote, "Speak to the professor or student assistant early if your team members don't do the work before the project is mostly completed."

In addition, three students had recommendations regarding the team leader role, suggesting "To have one person in charge of keeping things on track," and that "Someone has to take the initiative to ensure everything is set up to success and to ensure everyone is on the same page." Further, one student shared that future students should not be embarrassed to take on the leadership role, as stated in this comment, "For the most part, everyone is trying to get their points but don't want to take the lead, so you shouldn't worry about embarrassing yourself if you're the one that takes lead."

Summary of Student-Generated Strategies Used and Suggested Recommendations

Table 3 includes a summary of the strategies students shared they used and the recommendations they had for future students in the course to manage the challenges faced in virtual teams concerning communication, trust, connection and social bonding, and joint commitment and accountability.

DISCUSSION

Conclusion

This case study provides valuable information that can be used to develop further virtual team skills training for college-level students prior to entering the workforce. Along with a description of the design of the course and the virtual team assignments used in this case study, instructional strategies are shared that faculty may implement to assist students in managing the challenges of communication, trust, connection and social bonding, and joint commitment and accountability. While the authors hope these strategies will be transferable and useful in many college courses across various disciplines, faculty can draw from the instructional strategies presented in this case, test them out, and adapt them to their situations and courses.

Findings from the survey data revealed that allowing students to work in virtual teams within the context of an otherwise asynchronous online course allowed them to authentically develop their strategies to manage the challenges they may face while working remotely in the future. Although the students in this study did not receive any specific virtual team skills training at the beginning of the course, the results of this case study demonstrate that the students were able to effectively

TABLE 3

Summary of Student-Generated Strategies and Suggested Recommendations

Challenge	Strategies Used	Suggested Recommendations
Communication	• Created team communication norms in the team charter assignment. • Frequently used group messaging tools to send out updates and reminders. • Scheduled and held regular synchronous Zoom team meetings. • Emphasized constant and open communication.	• View communication as essential. • Emphasize constant and open communication. • Be vocal and use direct communication when dealing with unresponsive or underperforming team members.
Trust	• Created team accountability norms as a part of project and task management norms in the team charter assignment. • Created team norms for respectful, constructive, and inclusive decision-making.	• Be respectful and patient with team members and their schedules. • Be open-minded and flexible to individual team members' work styles. • Be open to working on a virtual team. • Keep the size of the virtual team small.
Connection and social bonding	• Helped and supported team members when they had questions.	• Have fun and enjoy the team's interactions and work. • Hold synchronous meetings to share individual team members' work habits, strengths, and weaknesses.
Joint accountability and commitment	• Used document-sharing application (Google Docs). • Created deadlines for early completion of work. • Assigned specific roles and delegated tasks to individual team members. • Reviewed and made use of clear assignment guidelines provided by the instructor.	• Develop an overall plan for the team's work. • Keep work organized. • Set deadlines and stay on top of them; strive to complete work ahead of course deadlines. • Hold team members accountable. • Strive to be on a team with reliable team members. • Do one's part of the team's work. • Assign individual team members clear roles and tasks. • Seek out assistance from a professor or student assistant when needed. • Consider having one member as the team leader to keep things on track.

meet these challenges by creating and implementing their emergent strategies to build resilient virtual teams (Kirkman & Stoverink, 2021). While students can be formally trained in how to work in virtual teams, research suggests that students may internalize their learnings far better when teachers offer authentic learning experiences to expose students to real-world problems and allow those same students to discover their own personalized and spontaneous strategies to solve the real-world challenges they face (Fairweather & Cramond, 2010; Nemiro et al., 2015; Sawyer, 2010).

To meet the *communication* challenge, students used various communication tools and realized the importance of consistent and open communication for virtual team success. While students were encouraged to communicate through asynchronous and synchronous forms of communication, they were given the freedom and autonomy to select their own set of tools for communicating with one another. Given that many students mentioned the use of Zoom team meetings as a way to accomplish their work, it was encouraging that students realized the importance of synchronous, rich forms of communication in virtual teamwork in order to form bonds within the context of an asynchronous class and to have a space to share and work through ideas. Group messaging tools were another frequent form of communication used. Intuitively, students realized that there were different purposes for each type of communication tool. Students used Zoom team meetings to generate ideas and for work sessions while sending reminders of assignment deadlines and meeting times through group messaging tools.

To meet the challenge of *joint commitment and accountability*, students developed strategies that would be transferable to any team situation, not just virtual teams, such as creating deadlines, striving to accomplish the work ahead of the deadlines, assigning roles, and delegating tasks to individual team members. This was encouraging, although students were not initially trained in using such techniques as task accountability charts (which might be something to include in the future). While accountability and an equitable workload are common challenges for university students working on team projects, the teams created their own unique set of accountability norms, including positive measures and consequences, in their team charters.

In this case study, fewer students mentioned strategies for building *trust, connection, and social bonding* within their teams. Of those that did, students shared that they had developed and implemented norms to encourage respect and inclusion of one another and helped and supported team members when they had questions. The virtual teams in this course were short-term project teams assembled to complete a joint project (Opdenakker & Cuypers, 2019). These ad hoc project teams are often made up of members with no preexisting working relationships who work together for a limited time and do not anticipate working together in the future (Thompson, 2014). The teams in this course may have been primarily task-focused, emphasizing actions to accomplish the team's work, and less relations-focused, where actions to develop social relations and connection between the members of the team would be emphasized (Fiedler, 1967; Henkel et al., 2019). Expanding the investigation to student virtual teams that work together for longer periods (i.e., long-term research or internship teams) might yield more specific strategies around the specific challenges of team trust and connection, and social bonding.

FUTURE DIRECTIONS

The current study's findings offer promising directions for developing virtual teaming skills in students. Allowing students to be exposed to the challenges of working in virtual teams and having to solve those challenges before having to do so in the workforce further prepares students for their future careers. However, a notable limitation of the course curriculum in which these students were enrolled was the absence of initial training on virtual team effectiveness. Future implementation should integrate more formalized virtual team training for students into the course curriculum.

To encourage the use of communication tools offered by the university to students (which would mean all students would have accessibility to these tools), initial training in these tools would be useful. Although some of the standard communication tools used by the students in the course were Cal Poly Pomona (CPP) tools (Zoom, Google Docs), some commonly used tools were not CPP-affiliated tools (GroupMe, text). Further, some tools offered to students at CPP (Microsoft Teams, Canvas Collaboration Tool) were not used. This may indicate the need for better preparation and training in university-sponsored communication tools as part of the curriculum for online courses. It would be helpful to include initial communication tool training, not only in how to use them but also in when it is most appropriate to use each tool and standard protocols to guide their usage.

Another form of training that may be useful would be some team bonding activity, required initially in the course for virtual team members to get to know each other and bond. The team building training should be done through rich mediums, such as Zoom, so that team members can see and hear one another simultaneously. This may help build swift trust (Meyerson et al., 1996) necessary for temporary virtual teams that only exist within the context of a single course and then disband after the course is over. The requirements in this class only had one team-building activity, and it was later in the semester. All the other virtual team requirements were task-focused.

In this case study, the students were all psychology majors enrolled in the same course on organizational psychology at Cal Poly Pomona, a university in Southern California. It would be helpful to expand research on virtual teams in higher education to other populations, including students from different majors (such as science, business, engineering, and the arts) and from students from across the globe. As one of the key benefits of virtual teams in business is to allow team members to join together no matter where they are located across the globe to solve organizational and societal problems (Nemiro, 2004; Nemiro, in press), expanding the study of global virtual teams in higher education is a necessary direction for future research.

REFERENCES

Allen, E., & Seaman, J. (2016). *Online report card: Tracking online education in the United States.* Babson Survey Research Group and Quahog Research Group. http://onlinelearningsurvey.com/reports/onlinereportcard.pdf

Ashforth, B. E., & Mael, F. (1989). Social identity theory and the organization. *Academy of Management Review, 14,* 20–39.

Bailey-Hughes, B. (2021). A communication audit exercise to enhance virtual team and individual communication skills. *Management Teaching Review, 6*(4), 298–308. https://doi.org/10.1177/23792981211001527

Brown, E. (2020, April 30). Could COVID-19 usher in a new era of working from home? *Knowable Magazine.* https://knowablemagazine.org/article/society/2020/could-covid-19-usher-new-era-working-home

Charteris, J., Berman, J., & Page, A. (2021). Virtual team professional learning and development for practitioners in education. *Professional Development in Education, 47*(4), 638–650.

Cleary, Y., & Slattery, D. (2009, August). *Virtual teams in higher education: Challenges and rewards for teachers and students* [Paper presentation]. AISHE International Conference Series (AISHE-C 2009), The National University of Ireland, Maynooth.

Cornella-Dorda, S., Garg, L., Thareja, S., & Vasquez-McCall, B. (2020, May). Revising agile teams after an abrupt shift to remote. In *The path to the next normal: Leading with resolve through the coronavirus pandemic* (pp. 86–93). McKinsey & Company.

Daft, R. L., & Lengel, R. H. (1986). Organizational information requirements, media richness, and structural design. *Management Science, 32*(5), 554–571. https://doi.org/10.1287/mnsc.32.5.554

Dans, E. (2020, December 30). Could 2021 be the year remote working becomes the new normal? *Forbes.* https://www.forbes.com/sites/enriquedans/2021/12/30/could-2021-be-the-year-remote-working-becomes-the-newnormal/?sh=14726674680b

Davis, A., & Zigurs, I. (2008). Teaching and learning about virtual collaboration: What we know and need to know. *AMCIS 2008 Proceedings, p. 168.* http://aisel.aisnet.org/amcis2008/168

Ellemers, N., Sleebos, E., & Stam, D. (2013). Feeling included and valued: How perceived respect affects positive team identity and willingness to invest in the team. *British Journal of Management 24*(1), 21–37.

Fairweather, E., & Cramond, B. (2010). Infusing creative and critical thinking into the curriculum together. In R. Beghetto & J. Kaufman (Eds.), *Nurturing creativity in the classroom* (pp. 113–140). Cambridge University Press.

Fiedler, F. (1967). *A theory of leadership effectiveness.* McGraw-Hill.

Flammia, M., Cleary, Y., & Slattery, D. (2016). *Virtual teams in higher education: A handbook for students and teachers.* Information Age Publishing.

Furamo, K., & Pearson, J.M. (2006). An empirical investigation of how trust, cohesion, and performance vary in virtual and face-to-face teams. *Proceedings of the 39th Hawaii International Conference on Systems Sciences,* Computer Society Press, Honolulu, HI.

Garro-Abarca, V., Palos-Sanchez, P., & Aguayo-Camacho, M. (2021, February 17). Virtual teams in times of pandemic: Factors that influence performance. *Frontiers in Psychology.* https://doi.org/10.3389/fpsyg.2021.624637

Goold, A., Augar, N., & Farmer, J. (2006). Learning in virtual teams: Exploring the student experience. *Journal of Information Technology Education, 5,* 477–490.

Grinnell, L., & Appunn, F. (2012). Virtual teams in higher education: The light and dark side. *Journal of College Teaching and Learning, 9*(1), 65–78. https://doi.org/10.19030/TLC.v9i1.6716

He, J., Wang, P., & Li, Z. (2008). Issues and best practices of virtual teamwork in the online learning environment. In *Proceedings of the 31st annual convention of the Association for Educational Communications and Technology (AECT)* (pp. 92–98). Research and Theory Division of AECT, Orlando, FL. https://members.aect.org/pdf/Proceedings/proceedings08/2008/08_11.pdf

Henkel, T., Marion, J., & Bourdeau, D. (2019). Project management leadership behavior: Task-oriented versus relationship-oriented. *Journal of Leadership Education, 18*(2), 1–14, https://doi.org/10.12806/V18/I2/R8

Jensen, S., & Trespalacios, J. (2022). Designing virtual teams for K–12 teachers. *The Journal of Applied Instructional Design, 11*(2). https://doi.org/10.51869/112/sjjt

Kentnor, H. E. (2015). Distance education and the evolution of online learning in the United States. *Curriculum and Teaching Dialogue, 17*(1 & 2), 21–34.

Kirkman, B. L., & Stoverink, A. C. (2021). Building resilient virtual teams. *Organizational Dynamics, 50*(1), 100825.

Kohut, G. F. (2012). Enhancing student collaboration in global virtual teams. *The Journal of Effective Teaching, 12*(3), 44–60.

Kulturel-Konak, S., Maurer, C. R., & Lohin, D. L. (2010). Teaching students how to effectively work in virtual teams. *International Journal of Information Technology Project Management, 1*(2), 61–78.

Logemann, M., Aritz, J., Cardon, P., Swartz, S., Elhaddaui, T., Getchell, K., Fleischmann, C., Helens-Hart, C., Li, X., Palmer-Silveira, J. C., Ruiz-Garrido, M., Springer, S., & Stapp, J. (2022). Standing strong amid a pandemic: How a global online team project stands up to the public health crisis. *British Journal of Educational Technology 53,* 577–592. https://doi.org/10.1111/bjet.13189

Mayfield, C. O., & Valenti, A. (2022). Team satisfaction, identity, and trust: A comparison of face-to-face and virtual student teams. *Active Learning in Higher Education.* https://doi.org/10.1177/14697874221118861

McKnight, A. (2021, June 21). Are you prepared to staff for the new normal? *Quad.com.* https://www.quad.com/resources/are-you-prepared-to-staff-for-the-new-normal/

Meyerson, D., Weick, K. E., & Kramer, R. M. (1996). Swift trust and temporary groups. In R. M. Kramer & T. R. Tyler (Eds.), *Trust in organizations: Frontiers of theory and research* (pp. 166–195). SAGE. https://doi.org/10.4135/9781452243610.n9

Nemiro, J. E. (in press). Virtual teams. In R. Reiter-Palmon & S. Hunter's (Eds.), *Handbook of organizational creativity* (2nd ed.). Elsevier.

Nemiro, J. E. (2004). *Creativity in virtual teams: Key components for success.* Pfeiffer/Wiley.

Nemiro, J. E. (2000). The glue that binds creative virtual teams. In Y. Malhotra's (Ed.), *Knowledge management and virtual organizations,* (pp. 101–123). Idea Group.

Nemiro, J., Larriva, C., & Jawaharlal, M. (2015). Developing creative behavior in elementary school students with robotics. *Journal of Creative Behavior, 51*(1), 1–26.

O'Connor, C., Mullane, K., & Luethge, D. (2021). The management and coordination of virtual teams in large classes: Facilitating experiential learning. *Journal of Management Education, 45*(5), 739–759. https://doi.org/10.1177/1052562921995550

Ocker, R. J. (2005). Influences on Creativity in asynchronous virtual teams: A qualitative analysis of experimental teams. *IEEE Transactions on Professional Communication, 48*(1), 22–39.

Opdenakker, R., & Cuypers, C. (2019). Effective virtual project teams: A design science approach to building a strategic momentum. *Future of business and finance.* Springer. https://doi.org/10.1007/978-3-030-22228-4_3

Rauer, J. N., Kroiss, M., Kryvinska, N., Engelhardt-Nowitzki, C., & Aburaia, M. (2021). Cross-university virtual teamwork as a means of internationalization at home. *The International Journal of Management Education, 19*(3), 1–13. https://doi.org/10.1016/j.ijme.2021.100512

Reiter-Palmon, R. (2021). Leading for team creativity: Managing people and processes. In A. S. McKay, R. Reiter-Palmon, & J. C. Kaufman (Eds.), *Creative success in teams*, (pp. 33–54), Academic Press. https://doi.org/10.1016/B978-0-12-819993-0.00003-5

Sanders, R., Mitchell, A., Wallace, P., Wood, D. D., & Brewer, P. (2015). Teaching and learning in cross-disciplinary virtual teams, *IEEE Transactions on Professional Communication, 58*(2), 208–229. https://doi.org/10.1109/TPC.2015.2429973

Sawyer, K. (2010). Learning for creativity. In R. Beghetto & J. Kaufman's (Eds.), *Nurturing creativity in the classroom,* (pp. 172–190). Cambridge University Press.

Stoian, C. E. (2020). Indirect vs. direct communication: Steps in becoming culturally intelligent. *Journal of Humanistic and Social Studies, 1*, 93–102. https://www.ceeol.com/search/article-detail?id=883309

Thompson, M. M. (2014, September). *Swift trust implications for government/comprehensive approach (WoG/CA) missions.* Defence Research and Development Canada Scientific Report DRDC-RDDC-2014-R79. https://apps.dtic.mil/sti/pdfs/AD1017672.pdf

Watson-Manheim, W. B., & Belanger, F. (2002). Support for communication-based work processes in virtual work. *e-ServiceJournal, 1*(3), 61–82

BOOK REVIEW

Artificial Intelligence and Learning Futures: Critical Narratives of Technology and Imagination in Higher Education, by Stefan Popenici

Reviewed by Rebecca McNulty
University of Central Florida

Popenici, S. (2022). *Artificial Intelligence and Learning Futures: Critical Narratives of Technology and Imagination in Higher Education,* 228 pp, Routledge. https://doi.org/10.4324/9781003266563

Artificial Intelligence and Learning Futures: Critical Narratives of Technology and Imagination in Higher Education critiques the evolution of artificial intelligence (AI) in educational technology. The author explores the historical definition of "intelligence" and uses that history to critically examine AI and the risks associated with its continued growth. Ultimately, the author concludes that the expansion of AI requires educators to reimagine technological priorities in educational spaces and how those priorities can be leveraged to support student learning.

This book was written by Stefan Popenici, Academic Lead for Quality Initiatives in Education Strategy at Charles Darwin University, Australia. Defined by the author, its purpose is "to explore some of the key areas that were ignored or remain superficially investigated in the enthusiasm for a technological revolution" (Popenici, 2022, p. 1). Rather than investigating the technical aspects of machine learning, the book explores various characteristics of artificial intelligence (AI) and their potential to affect educational technology (edtech) as well as student learning outcomes.

The introduction begins with an overview of the global crises that have dominated the beginning of the 21st century. Holistically, however, the book focuses on the "Americanisation of higher education" (Popenici, 2022, p. 73). While it expands to consider other countries and regions, its focus remains on American ideology and the trends it sets in edtech, which contribute to a field that is "Americanised in subtle and complex forms" (p. 1).

• **Correspondence concerning this article should be addressed to:** Rebecca McNulty, Rebecca.McNulty@ucf.edu

The Quarterly Review of Distance Education, Volume 24(1), 2023, pp. 79–81
Copyright © 2023 Information Age Publishing, Inc.

ISSN 1528-3518
All rights of reproduction in any form reserved.

After the introduction, the book is divided into three overarching sections, which are separated into nine chapters that examine the history of AI against reflections on the authors' personal experiences. The first section considers the ideology behind definitions of "intelligence," how that history has merged into mythologies that define "The American Dream," and how the two have combined to form narratives surrounding AI. The author also links intelligence research to eugenics and genocide, among other things. The second section explores AI in higher education, including considerations of automation, surveillance, and worldwide crises affecting student learning. The author also discusses the way AI has contributed to "significantly broadening the role of surveillance and data collection in education" (Popenici, 2022, p. 120). The third and final section imagines how AI might affect the future of higher education and how educators can re-imagine ways "to think for the common good, to speak truth to power, and to genuinely master critical thinking" (p. 145). In this way, the author also seeks to expose AI's influence into "the constant erosion of intellectual life in academia and excessive focus on quantitative criteria and various forms of exploitation," which the author calls "the open secrets of higher education" (p. 172). Ultimately, the book's conclusion returns to its introduction to "imagine and build sustainable solutions for the future," which require critical investigations into "how and if AI can help universities and students to avoid a dystopian future of continuous surveillance, control, and authoritarianism" (p. 6).

This book's strength lies in its comprehensive critical analysis of all components of AI, from its historical definitions to its potentials for growth as well as for harm. The author explores the challenges associated with building sustainable AI to support pedagogical best practices; he also discusses the systems and algorithms that contribute to a culture of surveillance in higher education. While the text is deeply critical of aspects of edtech, it showcases the ethical considerations that will be necessary for a wide-spread adoption of AI in the future. This content is especially relevant to academic leaders and administrators, who make decisions surrounding AI adoption, as well as to faculty, instructional technologists, and instructional designers, who are on the front lines of AI's future in higher education.

Published November of 2022, *Artificial Intelligence and Learning Futures* was released at the same moment that OpenAI launched the prototype of ChatGPT, a chatbot built on a large language model that generates unique text in response to user input (OpenAI, 2022). This publication date gives the text a unique perspective capturing an edtech landscape poised to become dominated by considerations of generative AI; however, this timeline also limits the author's consideration of the rapid affect this technology has had on higher education. Additionally, it is necessary to point out that while the author makes a convincing argument for the American ideological trends that have infiltrated many aspects of higher education across the world, a further analysis could include more explicit contrast of how other countries have approached AI in both policy and procedure.

Ultimately, this book takes a nuanced view of AI through the changing lens of higher education. It describes "the main failure of the university" to be one where imagination has been replaced with an "obsessive focus on big data, surveillance and predictive analytics, edtech gadgets, and software applications" (Popenici, 2022, p. 173). Instead, the author imagines a future of "new and courageous solutions, in a new paradigm, with new priorities and a rejection of education as a commodity with students as customers in a market" (p. 184). When explored through this lens, the author shows "the rise of AI" to be "just another reason to accept that this is the time when we must start to imagine" new approaches to higher education (p. 197). In this way, *Artificial Intelligence and Learning Futures* shows the way that educators will need to critically analyze AI to imagine both the risks and benefits that it might pose to the future of edtech and how that future will translate to new opportunities for student learning.

REFERENCES

OpenAI. (November 30, 2022). *Introducing ChatGPT*. OpenAI Blog. https://openai.com/blog/chatgpt

Popenici, S. (2022). *Artificial intelligence and learning futures: Critical narratives of technology and imagination in higher education.* Routledge. https://doi.org/10.4324/9781003266563

BOOK REVIEW

Hybrid-Flexible Course Design:
Implementing Student-Directed Hybrid Classes,
Edited by Brian J. Beatty (October, 2019, 254 pp.)

Reviewed by Mohsen Keshavarz
Torbat Heydariyeh University of Medical Science, Torbat Heydariyeh, Iran

INTRODUCTION

Dr. Brian J. Beatty wrote this book and it is a prominent book in the field of *Hybrid-Flexible Course Design*. The book was first published in 2019 as an e-book and this open textbook is offered under a CC-BY open content license and then it was edited for the first time by the author in May 2022, and due to the consequences of the Corona era in higher education, sections were added to it. The book has two formats, PDF and online, both of which can be downloaded for free on the Open Textbook Library site. The number of pages in the book is 254 pages. The book describes the fundamental principles of designing a HyFlex course and illustrates a process for design and implementation factors that faculty have experienced in various higher education institutions. Generally, this book introduces and provides the fundamental principles of the strategies, techniques, and methods of Hybrid-

Flexible (HyFlex) course design. The audience of this book is educational designers, educational managers and policymakers, educators/ faculty and students, and all people involved in the process of design of Hybrid-Flexible (HyFlex) courses. In general, after reading the book, readers gain useful knowledge and information about of Hybrid-Flexible (HyFlex) course and will be able to design and implement an of Hybrid-Flexible (HyFlex) course in response to special needs and challenges.

The book consists of three units. Unit I explains the subject of Hybrid-Flexible course design to support student-directed learning paths and gives a clear and comprehensive overview of HyFlex. Unit II state the implementation and adoption of Hybrid-Flexible and is about applying HyFlex, finally Unit III: covers the subject of Hybrid-Flexible implementations around the world and gives many

---

• Correspondence concerning this article should be addressed to: Mohsen Keshavarz, keshavarz_mohsen@yahoo.com

The Quarterly Review of Distance Education, Volume 24(1), 2023, pp. 83–86
Copyright © 2023 Information Age Publishing, Inc.

ISSN 1528-3518
All rights of reproduction in any form reserved.

useful examples related to applying it in various settings.

REVIEW OF THE BOOK

Generally, the book consists of three units and 22 chapters. Unit I: Hybrid-Flexible course design to support student-directed learning paths: chapters 1–4, Unit II: Implementation and adoption of Hybrid-Flexible instruction: Chapters 1–5, Unit III: Hybrid-Flexible implementations around the world: Chapters 1–13. The chapters of each unit are separate and do not run along with each other. The book reviewer used two approaches and methodologies to review the book. The first step we provided based on the descriptive approach the essential information about specifications, content, and structure of the book then presented the goals of each chapter. Finally, the key features are described in the conclusion section with an analytical and critical perspective the book reviewer tries to analyze the book for the first time. The chapters of unit 1 explain the reasons why hybrid-flexible courses and programs are offered. At the beginning of the book, Dr. Beatty tries to refer to the experience of San Francisco State University in hybrid-flexible courses

The author of the book describes the values and principles of hybrid-flexible course design. Dr. Beatty believes that fundamental values in hybrid-flexible design are as follows learner choice, equivalency, reusability, and accessibility and the HyFlex course design is built upon four fundamental values. He states that these values are the basis and based on which, goals, organizational strategies, and activities are drawn. For example, in the learner choice principle, students should have the right to choose among teaching methods in choosing how to participate in completing their academic activities.

The chapters in unit 2 emphasize how a Hybrid-Flexible course is created and established, and the author tries to reflect on the experiences and views of professors, students,

and professors in educational institutions These chapters reflect the experiences of The faculty in the field of in HyFlex and the author tries to portray their challenges and successes.

Dr. Beatty believes that four factors are very important from the experiences of professors and are effective in the effective teaching process. These four include (1) managing a multimodal learning environment, (2) workload, (3) student-instructor interaction, and (4) assessing learning progression.

Dr. Beatty state that we must be considered in HyFlex courses design to issues such as connecting students through common activities and shared experience, discussions drive connections among students, reflection discussions: a shared experience to connect students, reflection posts in practice, topical discussions: generative learning activities focused on course content, effective practices: overlapping discussions. The chapters in Unit III refer to the reports of universities and professors who have extensive practical experience in the field of Hybrid-Flexible courses in their environments. Each chapter describes how to design, implement, and evaluate Hybrid-Flexible courses. These reports and case studies provide a rich spectrum of Hybrid-Flexible courses that demonstrates a favorable approach and attitude to Hybrid-Flexible courses. In the following, we will try to briefly state the highlights of the chapters of Unit 3.

CONCLUSION

The reader can get a good view of the HyFlex approach and gain perspective and vision. This is a great resource for the reader who is attempting HyFlex implementation. The importance of the subject "HyFlex learning" in this book doubled during the COVID period.

If we want to point out a distinct feature of this book, we must say that the book is very appropriate for a text in a Hybrid-Flexible (HyFlex) course design. It covers a wide range of essential issues such as the values and principles of the Hybrid-Flexible course. The book consists of a regular format and structure. The initial units explain the basics of Hybrid-Flexible course design, and the final units focus on operational work and sample studies in this area, and each unit is divided into separate chapters. In addition, each chapter has its references and active access links. The book has valid and up-to-date scientific references, which gives students a foundation in theory and research in Hybrid-Flexible courses. It should also be noted that the subject of the book, entitled Hybrid-Flexible course design, is a new subject that has no history of extensive scientific research in this field and dates back to previous years, for this reason, this book is an outstanding work of its kind that has tried to explain its dimensions and components by focusing on the subject of Hybrid-Flexible.

I believe this book provides readers with strategies, methods, and case stories related to Hybrid-Flexible (HyFlex) course design so that audiences be able to make decisions in their environments with the HyFlex course (re)design. In explaining the concepts tries to use obvious practical examples with newer information in the field of Hybrid-Flexible, and this feature of the book "theory along with practical examples" distinguishes it from similar books. Structurally, diagrams, tables, and charts try to convey concepts to readers categorically and simply.

In my opinion, the order of presenting content from simple to difficult is one of the arts of the author in presenting the contents of the book.

Another interesting point of the book is the presentation of recorded educational videos with active access links to YouTube from students and faculty with experiences in the field of Flexible (HyFlex) course design, In my opinion, it can be interesting for the readers of the book and take them out of the monotony and boredom in reading the book

The author of the book is also a prominent person in this field. Dr. Brian Beatty works as an associate professor of instructional technologies in the Department of Equity, Leadership Studies, and Instructional Technologies at San Francisco State University. His areas of interest include social interaction in online learning, flipped classrooms, and developing instructional design theory for Hybrid-Flexible learning environments. Dr. Beatty is Known as a pioneer and leader in the development and evaluation of the HyFlex course design model for blended learning environments, at San Francisco State University. Dr. Beatty has more than 25 years of experience as a classroom teacher, trainer, and instructional designer at schools, businesses, and universities.

The principles and guidelines of this book are considered as a kind of instruction with the help of which policymakers in the field of Hybrid-Flexible learning environments make important decisions based on these principles and attempts have been made to properly separate the duties and responsibilities of, faculty and students, and institutions policymakers in the field of implementation of HyFlex course design.

The author of the book has tried to give examples of different types of HyFlex course design models in different sections of this book. These models help the readers of the book to get a conceptual picture of the desired topics. One of the salient features of the book, which is perhaps less seen in other examples, is explaining the topic by providing simple and multiple categories in the proposed areas. Another highlight of the book is the presentation of international research and case studies and information in the field of the HyFlex course. The author has tried to clarify the concept of the HyFlex course for the readers of the book by presenting a body of extensive research in the relevant field. I believe the author's goal was to say that the subject of the HyFlex course is an important and valuable subject that is being studied in many universities around the world.

The units and chapters of the book are very simple and fluent, the content is presented in general and in detail and a content sequence has been used. The language and expression of the book are simple and smooth. The book is not vague and confusing. The number of pages in each chapter is also short and does not bore the reader. The table of contents at the beginning of the book is a very useful guide for the reader, also the appendices are labeled and easily accessible and allow the readers to access other experts in the HyFlex field the authors of the book have used very attractive diagrams, figures, and graphs to describe and express the importance of the subject. One of the interesting points of this book is that in many of the projects and studies that the author reports as a case study, the author himself has acted as a consultant in these projects, which shows the author's mastery over the research done.

Another visible point of the book is chapter 13.3, which asks readers to share their research in this area with the author to be included in later edited versions of the book and has an ongoing call for case report chapter proposals, also, one of the attractive features of the book is that in addition to the theoretical topics, it has also considered assignments for the readers to become more familiar with the design of training courses in a practical way at the end of the chapters. It also provides examples and case reports from universities and faculty who have had successful experiences in the field of designing of Hybrid-Flexible to familiarize readers.

If we want to point out some of the weaknesses of the book, we must say that this book does not use many images and visual effects; perhaps this point has slightly reduced the appearance of the book, because compared to minted books in recent years, paying attention to photos and color images has a great impact on readers' learning, especially readers with visual learning styles. This is a well-crafted and organized text that is current and can aid in the adaption or adoption of a hybrid flex model of online education in higher education. In the end, it should be said that this book is a prominent, useful and, international book for researchers of hybrid and distributed learning.

REFERENCE

Beatty, B. J. (2019). *Hybrid-flexible course design: Implementing student-directed hybrid classes.* (1st ed.). EdTech Books. https://edtech-books.org/hyflex

CONFERENCE CALENDAR

Compiled by Vanaja Nethi
Nova Southeastern University

Below are some of the conferences on instructional technology, and online and blended learning that may be of interest to readers of the *Quarterly Review of Distance Education.*

USDLA 2023 National Distance Learning Week, November 7–11, 2023, Online + FREE

"The United States Distance Learning Association 2023 National Distance Learning Week conference will be streamed live on the Eduvision platform, in both English and Spanish. Registration is free and this week-long conference aims to generate greater awareness and appreciation for distance learning; celebrate distance learning applications in K–12, telehealth, higher education, corporate, and government/military; discuss current issues and emerging trends; highlight best practices; and recognize leaders in the field."
https://usdla.org/2023-ndlw/

International Conference on E-Learning and Online Education Technologies, December 27–28, 2023, Vienna, Austria

"International Conference on E-Learning and Online Education Technologies aims to bring together leading academic scientists, researchers, and research scholars to exchange and share their experiences and research results on all aspects of e-learning and online education technologies. It also provides a premier interdisciplinary platform for researchers, practitioners and educators to present and discuss the most recent innovations, trends, and concerns as well as practical challenges encountered, and solutions adopted in the fields of e-learning and online education technologies."
https://waset.org/e-learning-and-online-education-technologies-conference-in-december-2023-in-vienna

National Future of Education Technology Conference, January 23–26, 2024, Orlando, Florida

"For almost 50 years, The National Future of Education Technology ® Conference has brought together educators, administrators, and technology experts to discuss the latest advancements in education technology. The content presented at FETC is thoughtfully curated to provide professionals with actionable insights on what technology solutions to implement in their schools and districts. FETC

• **Correspondence concerning this article should be addressed to:** Vanaja Nethi, nethi@nova.edu

is the comprehensive source for education technology solutions, bringing together the best and brightest in the EdTech community for a collaborative and enjoyable exploration of pressing issues, new technologies, and best practices."
https://www.fetc.org/

TCEA Convention and Exhibition, February 3–7, 2024, Austin, Texas

"TCEA's Convention & Exposition attracts educators in every role in the field. Attendees come back to this conference year after year because they know they can expect to hear speakers who inspire, gather a ton of useful resources and strategies, meet vendors who will introduce them to possibilities and solutions, and have plenty of time to connect with other amazing educators. TCEA provides a transformative experience you won't forget."
https://convention.tcea.org/about/

ETC eLearning Annual Conference 2024, February 18–21, 2024, Las Vegas, Nevada

"The Instructional Technology Council (ITC) invites you to join us at eLearning to collaborate with colleagues from across the country and around the world, at one of the friendliest and most comprehensive annual conferences for eLearning practitioners. We want to learn about the new and innovative educational strategies and technologies you have implemented, and the tried-and-true techniques you or your staff use to teach at a distance. Have you experienced strategies that did not work out as well as you had hoped? We want to hear about the lessons you learned too."
https://www.itcnetwork.org/2024-annual-conference-elearning

DLAC 2024, February 26–28, 2024, Austin, Texas

"The Digital Learning Annual Conference (DLAC) celebrates online, blended, and digital learning practitioners and providers, and helps educators advance their schools, districts, and programs to their next attainable level. We are dedicated to serving those who are new to digital learning, while also remaining true to our roots as well. Educators in the early stages of using digital learning have findings to share, and even the most experienced educators using technology are constantly learning about how instruction, leadership, technology, and countless other factors interact. That's why we created DLAC mostly around sharing and networking, instead of around sitting and listening.
https://www.deelac.com/

Seventeenth International Conference on e-Learning & Innovative Pedagogies, March 7–8, 2024, Valencia, Spain + Online

"The e-Learning & Innovative Pedagogies Research Network is brought together around a common concern for new technologies in learning and an interest to explore possibilities for innovative pedagogies. We seek to build an epistemic community where we can make linkages across disciplinary geographic and cultural boundaries. As a research network we are defined by our scope and concerns and motivated to build strategies for action framed by our shared themes and tensions. The 2024 focus is on people, education, and technology for a sustainable future."
https://ubi-learn.com/2024-conference

Spring CUE 2024 Conference, March 21–23, 2024, Palm Springs, California

CUE (Computer Users in Education) is one of the oldest EdTech organizations. "Be inspired, connect with fellow educators, and learn about the latest ideas in teaching and learning and the best educational technology for your classroom! Spring CUE 2024 will be a celebration of Educators. It's time to come together and celebrate all that is good about being an educator. Spring CUE 2024 will feature hundreds of informative learning sessions, keynotes from thought leaders and renowned educators, hands-on experiences in eSports, AR/VR,

wellness, and more."
https://web.cvent.com/event/3d429dc4-
558c-4b13-b00e-a51f6a7ef127/
websitePage:d96aee74-d6aa-4c93-
8bcb-048abaf2c09e

SITE Conference 2024, March 24–29, 2024, Las Vegas, Nevada

"This Society for Information Technology and Teacher Education (SITE) Conference is the 35th annual conference. It is organized by the Association for the Advancement of Computing in Education an international nonprofit, educational organization with the mission of advancing information technology in education and e-learning research, development, learning, and its practical application. The conference is designed for educators from all disciplines, computer technology coordinators, K–12 administrators, curriculum developers, and others interested in improving education through technology."
https://www.aace.org/conf/

AUTHOR BIOGRAPHICAL DATA

Anel Ayala received a BA in psychology from Cal Poly Pomona. Ms. Ayala served as a research assistant to faculty in the psychology department, where she was involved with research focusing on virtual teams in higher education as well as on imagination inflation in a virtual paradigm setting. Ms. Ayala's current research interests are in work-life balance and in remote work, and beginning fall 2023, Anel will be attending the University of Nebraska Omaha to pursue a master's degree in industrial/organizational psychology.

Asmaa Benbaba is a lecturer of Arabic and Islamic Studies at the department of African and African-American Studies, University of Kansas. Her research interests include adult learning, online learning communities, online distance education learning environment in the foreign language classroom, English as a second language, second language acquisition, inclusive education, and quantitative and qualitative research methods.

Ritushree Chatterjee currently works as a learning experience designer at Amazon. She has managed and designed learning experiences across modalities of asynchronous online/blended/instructor-led trainings, incorporating learner-centric approaches, strategies, and technology. Her interests include SME-Designer partnerships, inclusivity in learning initiatives and evaluations. She has a masters in environmental science and a masters in edu-

cation specializing in curriculum and instruction and over 10 years of experience as a learning professional.

Nadia Jaramillo Cherrez is a senior instructional designer currently working at Oregon State University Ecampus. She advises faculty members from several disciplines (e.g., social sciences, education) in the development of online and hybrid courses that incorporate innovative, learner-centered pedagogical approaches and interactive technologies. Dr. Jaramillo Cherrez leads professional development webinars for the Quality Matters Instructional Designers Association. Her research involves several areas including instructional design, faculty and instructional designers' professional development, inclusive online teaching and critical pedagogies. She is also interested in online writing pedagogies and assessment design.

Darshana P. Juvale is currently working as an Instructional Design at the Poole College of Management at North Carolina State University. She has over 15 years of experience working in instructional design and instructional technologies for Iowa State University. She has experience in designing, developing, and facilitating faculty to design online and blended courses. She has collaborated with the faculty to help determine appropriate pedagogical approaches to asynchronous online courses following best practices and instructional design principles. Her professional interests include: instructional design, faculty development and blended/flipped learning approach. Darshana holds a master's degree in education with an emphasis on curriculum and instructional technology.

Mohsen Keshavarz has a PhD in virtual education planning. He is a faculty member in the of Department of E-Learning in Medical Sciences at Torbat Heydariyeh University of Medical Sciences now. His research interests include online and virtual learning, blended learning, telemedicine, new educational technologies, e-health, and multiple literacies in online environments. He has published several articles on virtual education in international journals such as IRRODL. He is an energetic advocate of distance learning in his home country of Iran, having translated Tony Bates's book *Teaching in a Digital Age* to Persian in addition to several other projects, some with international collaborators. He has recently been introduced by Leaders & Legends of Online Learning as an international figure in the field of online learning.

Jodee S. Lee received a BA from Cal Poly Pomona in psychology with a minor in management and leadership. While at Cal Poly Pomona, Ms. Lee served as a research and teaching assistant to faculty in the psychology department. Ms. Lee hopes to pursue graduate school in organizational psychology.

James Lindner is a professor at the Department of Curriculum and Teaching, College of Education at Auburn University. His research interests are agriscience education, career and technical education, distance education and its applications, quantitative and qualitative research methods.

Jill E. Nemiro is a professor of organizational psychology in the Psychology Department at Cal Poly Pomona. Dr. Nemiro's research interests in education focus on virtual team training for university students, the evaluation of programs that nurture in youth the development of prosocial values and long-term commitment to community service, and programs that support students and faculty in science, technology, engineering, and math-related disciplines. As an organizational psychologist, Dr. Nemiro has widely published on ways to design virtual teams to be collaborative, creative, and high performing organizational units. Before moving into academia, Dr. Nemiro worked as a film editor in the entertainment industry.

Chris Radcliffe has worked in education across a broad range of sectors, including K–12, postsecondary and higher education. His current role is as a school leader in an Australian K-12 distance education school. In addition to education, Chris's research areas include sustainable agriculture, indigenous knowledge, and postschool training.

Briseli San Luis received an associate of arts degree in psychology from Citrus Community College, and recently earned a BA degree in psychology from Cal Poly Pomona, where she served as a teaching assistant for a course on organizational psychology. Ms. San Luis hopes to pursue a master's degree in marriage and family therapy.

Michelle Wylie is the assistant dean of the public health (MPH) degree program at Chamberlain University's College of Health Professions. Wylie brings more than 15 years of experience to her role and specializes in faculty team development and public health services administration. Wylie also is a visiting professor at Menlo College in Atherton and teaches organizational behavior to undergraduate business students. Wylie recently presented at American Public Health Conference Poster Presentation: Interprofessional Collaboration, Integrative, Complementary and Traditional Complementary, and Traditional Health Practices: A Model Fostering Diversity, Equity, and Inclusion as Framed by

COVID-19. She also presented at the Association of Schools and Programs of Public Health on Engaging MPH Students and Alumni in an Interprofessional Collaborative Research Experience During the COVID-19 Pandemic: Structure, Process, and Outcomes Poster Presentation. She received the CHP Engagement Award in 2020, Chamberlain Ron Taylor Award in 2019, and the CMPH Chamberlain Care Award in 2019. Most recently, Wylie served as a supervisor for the University of San Francisco's population health sciences department. While at the University of San Francisco, she also served as a program assistant for the master of public health degree program. Wylie earned her doctor of education degree in the higher education leadership and management program at Walden University, master of public administration degree in health service administration from the University of San Francisco, and BA degree in history from the University of California, Los Angeles. She is a certified Six Sigma Yellow Belt.

Printed in the United States
by Baker & Taylor Publisher Services